Professional English

D0073935

English for Health Sciences

Martin Milner

Medical Review Board

Miguel Casas Arellano, MD
Faculty of Medicine, BUAP

Luis Guillermo Vázquez de Lara Cisneros, MD, PhD
Faculty of Medicine, BUAP

HEINLE
CENGAGE Learning

Australia · Brazil · Japan · Korea · Mexico · Singapore · Spain · United Kingdom · United States

English for Health Sciences
Martin Milner

Publisher, Global ELT: Christopher Wenger

Director of Product Development: Anita Radu-canu

Editorial Manager: Berta de Llano

Director of Product Marketing: Amy Mabley

International Marketing Manager: Ian Martin

Development Editor: Kylie Mackin

Assistant Development Editor: Josephine O'Brien

Editorial Assistant: Bridget McLaughlin

Production Project Manager: Chrystie Hopkins

Associate Production Editor: Erika Hokanson

Photo Researcher: Alejandra Camarillo

Illustrator: Ignacio (Iñaki) Ochoa Bilbao

Interior Design/Composition: Miriam Gómez Alvarado, Miguel Angel Contreras Pérez

Cover Design: Miriam Gómez Alvarado, Miguel Angel Contreras Pérez

Cover Images: © Comstock images / Alamy

Library of Congress Control Number: 2006901326

ISBN-13: 978-1-4130-2051-9

ISBN-10: 1-4130-2051-8

Heinle
25 Thomson Place
Boston, MA 02210
USA

Cengage Learning is a leading provider of customized learning solutions with office locations around the globe, including Singapore, the United Kingdom, Australia, Mexico, Brazil, and Japan. Locate your local office at: **international.cengage.com/region**

Cengage Learning products are represented in Canada by Nelson Education, Ltd.

Visit Heinle online at **elt.heinle.com**

Visit our corporate website at **cengage.com**

Photo Credits:

p.17, p.18, p.29, p.31, p.53, p.58, p.65, p.67, p.70: Photos.com/RF:

p.44: © BananaStock / Alamy

All other photos: © Comstock images / Alamy

Printed In the United States of America
4 5 6 7 8 9 10 10 09

Contents

To the Teacher   v

Unit 1   **Making a diagnosis**   1

          Lesson 1 So, what can I do for you   2

          Lesson 2 When did the problem begin   4

          Lesson 3 I'd like to examine you   6

          Lesson 4 What's the diagnosis   8

          Lesson 5 Let me explain your diet   10

          Lesson 6 To put it more simply   12

          Team Project 1   14

Unit 2   **Working under pressure**   15

          Lesson 1 If you are not sure, ask   16

          Lesson 2 He'll be fine, Mr Slenkovich   18

          Lesson 3 Has he ever fainted before   20

          Lesson 4 I'd like to ask you a few questions   22

          Lesson 5 We need to take a sample   24

          Lesson 6 Can I explain the procedure   26

          Team Project 2   28

Unit 3   **Breaking bad news**   29

          Lesson 1 Can you describe the pain   30

          Lesson 2 It's how you say it   32

          Lesson 3 It's getting you down, isn't it   34

          Lesson 4 We need a psychiatric evaluation   36

          Lesson 5 It might be multiple sclerosis   38

          Lesson 6 I'm afraid to say that…   40

          Team Project 3   42

Unit 4   **Calling in the Stroke Team**   43

Lesson 1 She can hardly speak   44

Lesson 2 How many fingers can you see   46

Lesson 3 We need to run a few more tests   48

Lesson 4 What medication would you prescribe   50

Lesson 5 Let's decide your rehabilitation plan   52

Lesson 6 I'm going to teach you some exercises   54

Team Project 4   56

Unit 5   **Referring a patient**   57

Lesson 1 I can't put up with the pain   58

Lesson 2 Thank you for referring the patient   60

Lesson 3 Let's examine your mouth   62

Lesson 4 Follow the postoperative advice   64

Lesson 5 Your test results are back   66

Lesson 6 You are very lucky   68

Team Project 5   70

Unit Reviews   72

Grammar Resource   77

Picture Dictionary   86

Glossary   92

Audio Script   97

Acknowledgements

We would like to thank the following educators who provided invaluable feedback throughout the development of **English for Health Sciences:** Marie-France Fortoul, CONALEP, Mexico; Eric M. Skier, Tokyo University of Pharmacy, Japan; Célia Sforcin Guimarães, ICBEU-Botucatu, Brazil; Silvia Verduzo Delgado, Prepa Contemporânea, Mexico; Yuan-Cheng Liu, National Taipei College of Nursing, Taiwan; Apaporn Chindaprasirt, Khon Kaen University, Thailand; Akiko Hagiwara, Tokyo University of Pharmacy and Life Science, Japan; Nancy Castro Crossley, DuocUC, Chile.

To the Teacher

English for Health Sciences is especially designed for students at the intermediate level who want to use their English for international communication in the fields of Health Science.

Objective

The purpose of this book is to empower students with the language and life skills they need to reach their career goals. Students are exposed to real life situations that enable them to use the language in meaningful ways. The integrated skills approach develops the student's self-confidence to succeed in professional and social encounters within an English-speaking global community.

Content

English for Health Sciences has been designed with a core of 30 lessons plus additional resource sections to provide teachers and course designers with the necessary flexibility to plan a wide variety of courses.

The four skills of listening, speaking, writing, and reading are developed throughout each unit in professional contexts.

Students and practicing professionals will immediately be motivated by the opportunity to practice their English language skills in the following job-related situations:

Diagnosing

Putting a patient at ease with small talk, taking a medical history, asking open-ended questions, presenting a case, and explaining medical examinations and procedures to a patient

Treating a patient

Giving advice, explaining a case to a relative, explaining causes and treatments, giving discharge instructions, and calming people down

Dealing with difficult cases

Describing and identifying causes of pain, being supportive, presenting a case in lay as well as medical terms, and breaking bad news

Planning rehabilitation and long-term care

Examining a non-verbal patient, communicating with the next of kin, explaining test results to patient and relatives, explaining the characteristics of long-term care, and giving instructions for physical therapy

Referring a patient

Calling in a specialist, referring a patient to another doctor for tests and / or treatment, and giving postoperative advice

Using the book

The five content-based units in **English for Health Sciences** are divided into six two-page lessons. Each lesson is designed to present, develop, and practice a particular job-related skill. (See **Content**)

Vocabulary

The content vocabulary that might be unfamiliar to an intermediate-level student is marked with an asterisk. The definitions of these words appear in alphabetical order, by unit, in the glossary at the back of the book.

Common technical vocabulary (e.g. surface anatomy, instruments, simple procedures) is illustrated in the picture dictionary at the back of the book. These words are also recorded on the audio CD for pronunciation practice.

Grammar

There is no direct grammar instruction in the core lessons. However, a complete grammar resource has been provided at the end of the book. The grammar resource can be utilized in various ways according to the specific needs of each class group. It can serve as a reinforcement of the student's grammar skills and thus be used for self-study or independent practice. Alternatively, the teacher may choose to use this material in class to present and practice language skills required in the productive exercises throughout the book.

The language elements are ordered as they would appear in a traditional grammar syllabus, but they may be referred to in any order. Each of these topics is composed of a *grammar box* or explanation followed by contextualized examples and practice exercises.

Listening

Many of the workplace situations described are presented and / or established through the listening contexts. Complete audio scripts and an audio CD have been provided for the student to allow for independent listening practice. Student access to audio scripts and CDs also provides multi-level instruction opportunities in the classroom.

On-going assessment

The team projects in each of the five units as well as the one-page unit reviews at the end of the book provide ample opportunity for on-going assessment. Unit tests are provided in the Teacher's Resource Book.

Unit 1

Making a diagnosis

So, what can I do for you

a Do you agree or disagree with the following statements. Compare your answers with those of a classmate and discuss the reasons for your choice.

When taking a medical history, you should...	Agree	Disagree
1. try to ask as many open-ended questions as possible.	☐	☐
2. ask questions like, "And I assume you also have headaches, don't you?"	☐	☐
3. take notes as you are interviewing the patient	☐	☐

b Put these steps for taking a patient's history into the correct order. Compare your answers with those of a partner.

☐ Chief Complaint
☐ Family History
☐ History of Present Condition
☐ *1* Introductory "small talk"
☐ Medication
☐ Past Medical History
☐ Physical Examination
☐ Social History

c Work in groups. Discuss the following questions.

1. What is the purpose of making "small talk" at the beginning of a consultation?
2. What topics might be suitable for making "small talk"?

d Decide if the following ways of making "small talk" are good or bad. Compare your answers with those of a partner.

	Good	Bad
1. You're not looking very well, Mrs. Gray.	☐	☐
2. How's the new house, Mr. Roper?	☐	☐
3. Are you still playing basketball, Mark?	☐	☐
4. How's work going, Mrs. Gomez? Are you still with the insurance company?	☐	☐
5. Have you stopped smoking yet, Mrs. Ellingson?	☐	☐

e Write five more "small talk" questions.

1. _____

2. _____

3. _____

4. _____

5. _____

f Walk around the class and make "small talk" with the other students.

g Circle the best option, **a** or **b** to ask about the chief complaint. Compare your answers with those of a partner.

1. a) So, what brings you here today?   b) So, what brings you here today, Mrs. Wright?

2. a) OK then, so, what's the problem?   b) What's the problem?

3. a) OK, tell me what the problem is.   b) OK, tell me everything you can about the problem.

4. a) Right, shoot!   b) Right, let's begin.

5. a) Well, what can we do for you?   b) Well, what can I do for you?

h Listen to Dr. Murray and Robert, the medical intern, doing a consultation. Evaluate the first part of the consultation.

CD T-2

	Very good	**OK**	**Poor**
1. Small talk			
2. Opening question			
3. Allowing patient to speak			

> **Communication Tip**
>
> Studies have shown that doctors interrupt their patients, on average, after only 18 seconds of the interview. Give patients a chance to say what they have to say. There will be time for your questions later.

i Listen to the rest of the conversation and complete Robert's notes. Which steps in taking a medical history are not covered in the consultation?

CD T-3

Patient: Mark Thurston

Age: 13

Chief complaint: (1)   *Excessive thirst* _____

History of present condition

    onset and timing: (2)   *Two or three weeks ago, after meals/eating* _____

    other symptoms: (3) _____

    previous occurrence: (4) _____

Past medical history: (5) _____

Medication: (6) _____

Social history: (7) _____

Family history: (8) _____

Lesson 2

When did the problem begin

a Match the questions with the steps for taking a patient's history.

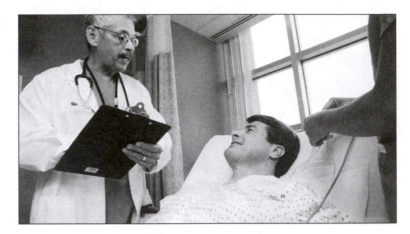

Questions

a. _3c_ Have you had similar problems before?
b. ____ When did the problem begin?
c. ____ Are you having any other pain or problems?
d. ____ Are you taking any medication?
e. ____ Are you a smoker?
f. ____ So, how can we help you today?
g. ____ Has anyone in your family had a similar problem?
h. ____ Are you allergic to any medication?
i. ____ Have you ever had any other medical problems?
j. ____ Do you have a job that involves a lot of exercise?
k. ____ How's the rest of the family?

Steps

1. Introductory "small talk"
2. Chief Complaint
3. History of present condition
   a) onset and timing
   b) other symptoms
   c) previous occurrence

4. Past Medical History
5. Family History
6. Medication
7. Social History

b Rewrite the following leading questions so they are more open-ended.

1. I imagine the pain stops you from working, doesn't it?
   Does the pain interfere with your daily life?
2. And I suppose you get terrible back pains as well?
   _____
3. I don't suppose you get indigestion after you eat bread, do you?
   _____
4. I expect you don't know much about celiac disease* do you?
   _____
5. I presume you have a healthy balanced diet.
   _____
6. So, I assume you get stabbing* pains in your chest after exercise, don't you?
   _____
7. I'm sure you've been losing weight as well.
   _____

> ● **Communication Tip**
>
> Avoid leading questions. Leading questions direct the patient to the answer that the doctor, maybe subconsciously, wants to hear. Always try to ask open-ended questions so that the patient expresses the problem in their own words. Avoid words like: assume, presume, suppose, expect, imagine, sure.

c Write the doctor's questions in the dialogue. Then practice the interview with a partner.

Doctor: (1) _So, how can I help you?_
Patient: I have a really bad earache.
Doctor: (2) _____
Patient: No, it is only in my left ear.
Doctor: (3) _____
Patient: It started about two weeks ago.
Doctor: (4) _____
Patient: No, some days it's not so bad.
Doctor: (5) _____
Patient: Yes, sometimes I get headaches as well.
Doctor: (6) _____
Patient: No, I have never had an earache like this before.

 d Role-play taking medical histories of the following cases.

Case 1

Name: Charmine Plantz
Occupation: Sales manager
Age: 31
Medication: None
Chief Complaint: Painless lump* on the front of the neck for one month
Other symptoms: Losing weight, always hungry, rapid heartbeat, hot flushes,* diarrhea

Case 2

Name: Selina Burton
Occupation: Typist
Age: 37
Chief Complaint: Tingling* of first three fingers and thumb that gets worse at night
Other symptoms: Weakness of fingers (has difficulty buttoning clothes), sometimes pain in forearm

Case 3

Name: Bob Smithson
Occupation: Construction worker
Age: 50
Chief Complaint: Attacks of dizziness* with nausea and vomiting. During attack, high pulse rate and rapid breathing. No pattern to attacks
Other symptoms: Hissing* in ears (on both sides), loss of hearing

Case 4

Name: Chuck Talavera
Occupation: Farmer
Age: 38
Chief Complaint: Cough with bad tasting phlegm*
Other symptoms: Low fever, night sweats,* weight loss
Social History: Long-term smoker

Lesson 3

I'd like to examine you

a Add more words or expressions to the charts.

Could you stand up, please?

I am just going to take your temperature.

Requesting		
Would you Could you If you could	stand up, stand here, lie down, sit up, breathe in, breathe out, take off your shirt, relax, roll up your shirt sleeve, go to the bathroom and fill this jar, _____ _____ _____ _____ _____	please?

Explaining procedures	
I am (just) going to I'd (just) like to	take your temperature. weigh you. take some blood for testing. _____ _____ _____ _____

CD
T-4

b Listen to the conversation and fill in Robert's notes

Patient: Mark Thurston

Age: 13

Height: _____

Weight: _____

Temperature: _____

Blood pressure: _____

Pulse: _____

Respiration rate: _____

Head and Neck

    Eyes: _____

    Ears: _____

    Mouth: _____

    Neck: _____

c Dr. Murray is talking to Robert about Mark's case. Fill in the blanks in their dialogue using words from the box.

diagnosis
complaining
blood
reports
history
enlargement
thyroid

Dr. Murray: So, Robert, let's run through the case. Can you summarize it for me?

Robert: OK. We have a thirteen-year-old male (1) _____ of excessive thirst with polyuria *, especially after meals. He also (2) _____ that he feels lethargic. There might be a family (3) _____ of diabetes mellitus. The patient has a Body Mass Index of 17.5, which indicates that he is underweight. On examination, pulse, temperature, blood pressure, and respiration rate were normal. There was an (4) _____ of the thyroid gland. I would make an initial (5) _____ of Type 1 Diabetes Mellitus.

Dr. Murray: Very good. I would agree with you. So what lab tests would you run?

Robert: I think we need a urine glucose test and a fasting* (6) _____ glucose test. In addition, I think we ought to do a (7) _____ function test, and a urine ketone* test. We could also do an oral glucose tolerance test.

d Work in groups. Present summaries of the following cases using medical language.

Case 1
Name: Charmine Plantz   **Age:** 31
Occupation: Sales Manager
Chief Complaint: Lump* on front of neck for one month
Other symptoms: Palpitations. Heat intolerance. Nervousness. Insomnia. Breathlessness.* Increased bowel movements. Light menstrual periods.
Physical examination: Enlarged thyroid, Tachycardia.* Slight hypertension. Warm, moist, smooth skin. Exophthalmus.* Tremor.* Weight loss. Muscle weakness. Hair loss.

Case 2
Name: Selina Burton   **Age:** 37
Occupation: Typist
Chief Complaint: Tingling of first three fingers and thumb that gets worse at night
Other symptoms: Weakness of fingers (has difficulty buttoning clothes). Sometimes pain in forearm.
Physical examination: Muscle wasting* at base of thumb. Unable to distinguish hot from cold.

Case 3
Name: Bob Smithson   **Age:** 50
Occupation: Construction worker
Chief Complaint: Attacks of dizziness with nausea and vomiting. During attack, high pulse rate and rapid breathing. No pattern to attacks.
Other symptoms: Hissing or ringing* in ears (on both sides), loss of hearing
Physical examination: Vital signs* normal. Nystagmus.* Positive Romberg test.*

Case 4
Name: Chuck Talavera   **Age:** 38
Occupation: Farmer
Chief Complaint: Low subjective fever, cough with bad tasting phlegm, night sweats,* and weight loss getting worse over the last four months
Social History: Long-term smoker
Physical examination: Temperature of 38°C, gingival disease, dullness* to percussion and absent breath sounds in lower right lobe* of lung. Clubbing* of fingers.

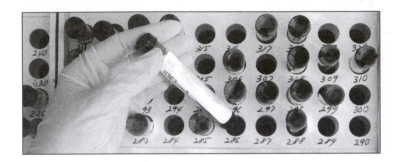

Fasting Blood Glucose Level:	142 mg/dl	(Normal range 70 - 110 mg/dl)
Glucose Tolerance Test (75gm)	210 mg/dl after 2 hours	(Normal range less than 140 mg/dl)
Glucosuria*	Positive	
Thyroid Function	Serum Thyroxin of 12 mg/dl	(Normal Range 7-12 mg/dl)

a Fill in the blanks in the sentences below using words from the box.
Then number the sentences to make a conversation.

results	limits	priority	diagnosis	comprehensive	treatment

☐ **Robert:** It looks likes we were correct with our preliminary (1) _____ of diabetes.

☐ **Robert:** That sounds good to me. Now, where do we begin with the (2) _____ of the diabetes?

☐ **Dr. Murray:** That's right. But what do you think about the thyroid result?

☐ **Dr. Murray:** Well, I think the first (3) _____ is to get the diabetes under control and then we can monitor the thyroid.

☑ **Dr Murray:** Hi, Robert. Have you seen Mark Thurston's lab test (4) _____? What do you think?

☐ **Dr. Murray:** Well, the first step is to draw up a (5) _____ treatment plan.

☐ **Robert:** Well, it's just within the (6) _____ but I think we ought to do a more comprehensive thyroid review.

b Below are the elements of Mark's treatment plan. Classify them as either *immediate actions (I), ongoing actions (O),* or *both (B).*

___ 1. Train patient to monitor blood sugar levels

___ 2. Have annual eye check

___ 3. Monitor thyroid function

___ 4. Visit nutritionist

___ 5. Visit podiatrist*

___ 6. Train patient to give insulin injections

___ 7. Instruct patient, patient's family, and school staff to recognize and treat hypoglycemia*

___ 8. Arrange psychological counseling (if necessary)

___ 9. Have annual dental check

___ 10. Run hemoglobin A1C test*

c Before you listen to Dr. Murray explaining the diagnosis of diabetes, think of three questions that Mrs. Thurston and Mark might ask the doctor. How do you think Dr. Murray will answer?

Questions from Mrs. Thurston and Mark	Answers from Dr. Murray
1. *Mark: Will I still be able to play basketball?*	*Yes, of course.*
2. _____	_____
3. _____	_____
4. _____	_____

CD T-5

d Listen and write down five points that Dr. Murray told Mark and his mother.

1. _____
2. _____
3. _____
4. _____
5. _____

e Role-play the following situations.

1.
Student A: Robert
Student B: Mark
Task: Robert has to explain to Mark how to recognize and treat mild hypoglycemia in simple, non-medical language.
Signs and symptoms of mild hypoglycemia
Anxiety, tremors, hyperhidrosis* polyphagia*, nausea, tachycardia, mental confusion or difficulty concentrating, vertigo*, headache.
Treatment
As soon as the symptoms have been recognized, it is essential to raise blood sugar level. This can be done by ingesting 15 to 20 grams of carbohydrate. This is equivalent to 6 ounces of cola, or 4 glucose tablets.
It will take about 10 to 15 minutes for the blood sugar level to rise to normal.

2.
Student A: Mrs. Thurston
Student B: Robert
Task: Robert has to explain to Mrs. Thurston how to recognize and treat severe hypoglycemia in simple, non-medical language.
Signs and symptoms of severe hypoglycemia
Dysarthria*, disorientation, confusion and irrational behavior, loss of consciousness, seizures.*
Treatment
Severe hypoglycemia is potentially life-threatening and treatment should be immediate. Treatment for the unconscious patient is an intramuscular injection of glucagon. Patients whose blood glucose is not well controlled are advised to carry an injection kit that contains glucagon.
If there is no response to treatment, then emergency personnel should be alerted.

Lesson 5

Let me explain your diet

a Read the text and answer the questions below.

Refined Sugar in the Diabetic Diet

Before insulin was discovered in the 1930s, it was possible to treat Diabetes Mellitus Type 1 by strictly controlling carbohydrates in the diet. Refined* sugar was prohibited because it was thought that it raised blood glucose level to dangerous levels. However, in 1994, a committee for the American Diabetes Association, or ADA, published a paper that indicated that there was little experimental evidence to support this position. They pointed out that sugar is a form of carbohydrate and all carbohydrates contain approximately the same amount of energy. So, if a patient eats 100 grams of sugar or 100 grams of

unrefined carbohydrates like rice or potatoes, the amount of glucose entering the blood will be almost the same. Therefore the *amount* of carbohydrate in the diet is important, not necessarily the *type* of carbohydrate. However, it should be borne in mind that unrefined carbohydrates also contain proteins, etc., which are important in a balanced diet.

The important points to remember are that the patient's diet should contain the right number of calories for his or her individual needs and that the diet should be well- balanced.

1. Before the 1930s, how was diabetes treated?
2. On what grounds did the ADA change its policy on refined sugar?
3. If a patient asked you if it was all right to substitute 100 grams of candy for 100 grams of potatoes, what would you say?
4. Should unrefined carbohydrates in the form of sugar be prohibited from a diabetic diet?

b Put these pieces of advice in the correct columns.

- Eat three regular meals per day.
- Make sure you eat enough proteins in the form of meat, cheese, eggs, etc.
- Don't eat a whole packet of cookies at one time.
- Don't miss a meal.
- Try to avoid fast food.
- Eat lots of non-starchy vegetables.

Principle 1: Keep your blood sugar at a steady level	Principle 2: Eat a balanced diet
Eat three regular meals per day.	

c A nutritionist is explaining to Mark and his mother how to calculate the calories in his diet. Put these steps in the correct order. Then listen and check your answers.

CD
T-6

- [ ] ____ Adjust his diet so that he is getting about 2250 calories.
- [ ] ____ Calculate how many calories there are in one of his mom's servings.
- [ ] ____ Check that he is getting a balanced diet.
- [ ] ____ Weigh his mom's servings.
- [ ] ____ Add up the number of calories he eats per day.
- [ ] ____ Check how many calories there are in a regular serving from the chart.

d Do some of Mark's calculations.

Serving	Size of regular serving	Calories per regular serving	Size of Mark's mom's servings	Calories in one of Mark's mom's servings
1. Cornflakes	35g	130 cals	70g	*70/35 x 130 = 260cals*
2. Spaghetti	300g	300 cals	450g	
3. Rice	300g	420 cals	400g	
4. Boiled potatoes	300g	210 cals	500g	
5. Oatmeal	350g	175 cals	400g	

e Look at these two ways of regulating a diet. Explain them to your partner in your own words. Make sure your partner has understood.

● **Communication Tip**

As we have already seen, patients do not remember everything they are told. One way to help them remember is to repeat and summarize what you say at the end of the consultation. Another way is to have the patients themselves do this repetition and summary.

1. Student A explains to Student B

It can be time consuming and complicated to calculate the calories in every meal. Here is a much quicker method.

If you know how many calories there are in, say, a serving of meat with 1 small potato, you can use the information in the chart below and substitute 1 small potato for 1/3 cup of boiled rice. You have a math free way to vary your diet!

The following servings all contain about the same number of calories, so the diabetic patient can substitute one for another in a meal.

1 slice of bread
1/2 English muffin, bun, small bagel, or pita bread
1/2 cup cooked cereal, pasta
1/3 cup boiled rice
1 slice of bread
1/2 cup sweet potatoes
1/2 cup corn kernels, peas

2. Student B explains to Student A

There is no such thing as a special diabetic diet. Diabetic patients can eat the same type of food as the rest of their family. They just have to control how much they eat and when they eat. The essential principle is that they follow a balanced diet and to do this they can refer to the food pyramid. Another useful way to balance the diet is the "plate method." This method is described here.

The Plate Method.

2/5 of plate to be filled with starchy foods like rice, pasta, potatoes, etc.
2/5 of plate to be filled with fruits and vegetables
1/5 of plate to be filled with meat, fish and chicken, etc.

Lesson 6

To put it more simply

a The following words all appear in the article below. Use the article and the chart below to work out their meaning.

1. euthyroidism   *normal thyroid function*
2. hypothyroidism _____
3. dyslipidemia   _____

4. glycemic   _____
5. glucogenesis _____

Diabetes and Hyperthyroidism

The presence of thyroid dysfunction may affect diabetes control. Hyperthyroidism is typically associated with worsening glycemic control and increased insulin requirements. There is underlying increased hepatic glucogenesis, rapid gastrointestinal glucose absorption, and probably increased insulin resistance. Indeed, thyroid dysfunction may unmask latent diabetes.

In diabetic patients with hyperthyroidism, physicians need to anticipate possible deterioration in glycemic control and adjust treatment accordingly. Restoration of euthyroidism will lower blood glucose level.

Hypothyroidism is accompanied by a variety of abnormalities in plasma lipid metabolism, including elevated triglyceride and low-density lipoprotein (LDL) cholesterol concentrations. Even sub-clinical hypothyroidism can exacerbate the coexisting dyslipidemia commonly found in type 2 diabetes and further increase the risk of cardiovascular diseases. Adequate thyroxine replacement will reverse the lipid abnormalities.

Prefix		Root		Suffix	
hyper-	too high	*-glyc-*	sugar	*-ism*	noun
hypo-	too low	*-em-*	blood	*-ic*	adjective
eu-	normal	*lipid*	fat	*-ia*	noun
dys-	abnormal	*-ur-*	urine	*-genesis*	production

b Use the chart to work out the meaning of these words.

1. euglycemia   _____
2. hyperlipidemia _____

3. hyperglycosuria _____
4. dysuria   _____

c Listen to Doctor Murray explaining the main points of the article "Diabetes and Hyperthyroidism" to Mark. Write examples of the techniques he uses to simplify and explain.

CD T-7

Techniques	Examples
Uses analogies.	1. *The car analogy. Accelerator, gas, brake.*
Encourages Mark to ask questions.	2.
Checks if Mark is understanding.	3.
Asks Mark to repeat what he has learned.	4.
Is positive.	5.

d Read the following article. Highlight the parts that are relevant to Mark's case. Then write some notes in non-technical English that could be used to explain the Hemoglobin A1C test to him.

Hemoglobin HA1C Test

Background

A1C, also known as glycated hemoglobin or glycosylated hemoglobin, indicates a patient's blood sugar control over the last 2-3 months. A1C is formed when glucose in the blood binds* irreversibly to hemoglobin to form a stable glycated hemoglobin complex. Since the normal life span of red blood cells is 90-120 days, the A1C will only be eliminated when the red cells are replaced; A1C values are directly proportional to the concentration of glucose in the blood over the full life span of the red blood cells. A1C values are not subject to the fluctuations that are seen with daily blood glucose monitoring.

The A1C value is an index of mean* blood glucose over the past 2-3 months but is weighted* to the most recent glucose values. Values show the past 30 days as ~50% of the A1C, the preceding 60 days giving ~25% of the value and the preceding 90 days giving ~25% of the value. This bias* is due to the body's natural destruction and replacement of red blood cells. Because red cells are constantly being destroyed and replaced, it does not take 120 days to detect a clinically meaningful change in A1C following a significant change in mean blood glucose.

Clinical Utility

The American Diabetes Association (ADA) recommends A1C as the best test to find out if a patient's blood sugar is under control over time. The test should be performed every 3 months for insulin-treated patients, during treatment changes, or when blood glucose is elevated. For stable patients on oral agents* the recommended frequency is at least twice per year.

The Diabetes Control and Complications Trial and the United Kingdom Prospective Diabetes Study studies showed that the lower the A1C number, the greater the chances to slow or prevent the development of serious eye, kidney and nerve disease. The studies also showed that any improvement in A1C levels can potentially reduce complications.

The ADA recommends that action be taken when A1C results are over 8%, and considers the diabetes to be under control when the A1C result is 7% or less.

Source: http://www.metrika.com/3medical/hemoglobin-m.html

_____
_____
_____
_____
_____

e Role-play an explanation about Hemoglobin A1C to Mark. Use your notes from exercise **d**.

f Think of another highly technical subject that you are familiar with. First, explain it in simple, non-technical language to your group and then give a technical explanation.

CHILDHOOD AND ADOLESCENT ILLNESSES

Children and adolescents are particularly susceptible to a large number of medical disorders. Their immune system is not as developed as that of adults, and indeed it is normal for young children to have six to eight upper respiratory tract infections and two or three gastrointestinal infections each year.

In addition, congenital disorders often begin to show up in early life. Moreover, the active nature of children and adolescents means that they are more likely to be involved in accidents.

A Research Phase

Work in groups and research first aid for ONE of the following childhood or adolescent illnesses:

- Infectious diseases: (measles, mumps, chicken pox, pertussis, rubella, diphtheria, etc.)
- Nocturnal enuresis
- Infectious mononucleosis
- Osgood-Schlatter disease
- Scoliosis
- Eczema

Useful Key Words	
child	disease
children	disorders
infant	condition
juvenile	pediatrics
illness	

B Presentation Phase

- Present your findings to the class.
- Use pictures or charts / posters to make your presentations more interesting.

Unit 2

Working under pressure

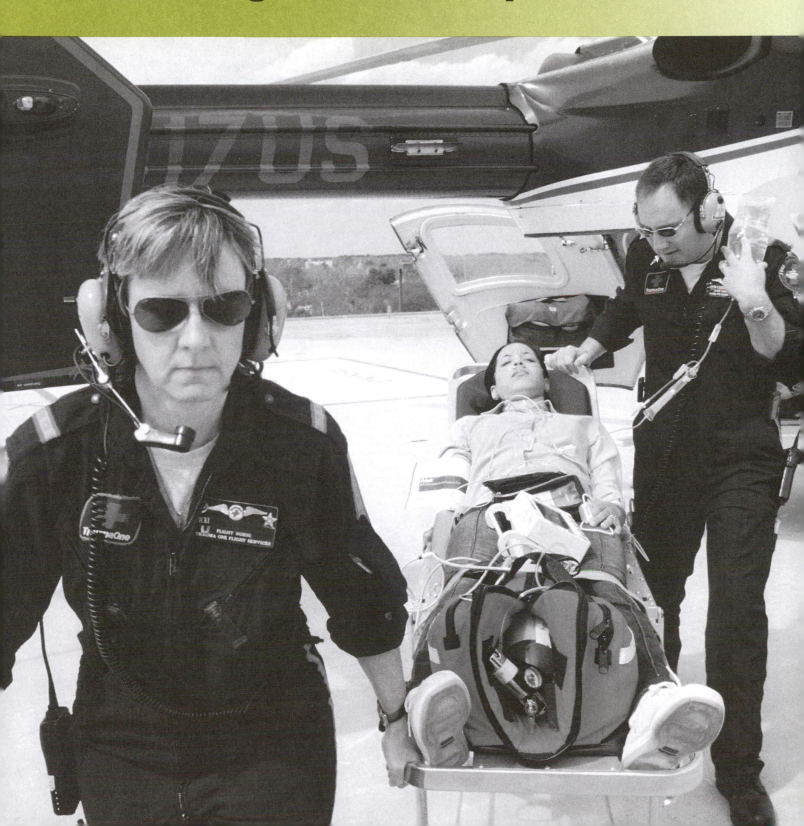

If you are not sure, ask

a Robert is about to start work in the Emergency Department with Dr. Jenny Tan. Write some advice you would give him for working in these stressful conditions.

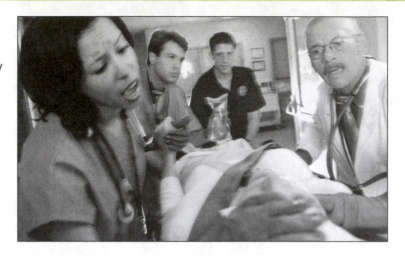

_____

_____

_____

_____

b Listen to the conversation between Robert and Jenny. Write the advice Jenny gives Robert. Then compare her advice with yours.

CD
T-8

1. _____

2. _____

3. _____

4. _____

5. _____

MEDICAL SCREENING EXAM

Patient: **Wayne Slenkovich** .... Age: **34** ....

CHIEF COMPLAINT: **Assault. Struck on the head. Unable to close mouth.**

Vital signs: **BP 120/80** Respiration rate: **20** Pulse rate: **20** Temperature: **37°C**

Mental status: **Conscious on arrival. Witnesses report him being unconscious for about 10 minutes after the attack.**

General appearance: **Slightly confused. Responds to questions.**

Ability to walk: **Ambulant**

TRIAGE STATUS: **Category III**

CD T-9

c Read the telephone conversation between Robert and Dr. Plantz, the dental intern. Number the lines in the correct order. Then listen and check your answers.

1 **Robert:** Hello, is that Doctor Plantz?

☐ **Dr. Plantz:** Morning, Robert. What can I do for you?

☐ **Robert:** We have a patient here with head injuries and a possible mandibular* fracture. Could you come down and have a look?

☐ **Robert:** Good morning, doctor. This is Robert Mitchell from Emergency.

☐ **Robert:** About fifteen minutes. Sure. Bye.

☐ **Dr. Plantz:** Sure, but I'm just finishing a ward round.* Is the patient stabilized?

☐ **Dr. Plantz:** Speaking.

☐ **Dr. Plantz:** No, stabilized! I mean, can you wait about a quarter of an hour?

☐ **Robert:** Sorry, I missed that. What did you say? Sterilized?

> ● **Communication Tip**
>
> Using the telephone in a foreign language is not easy. Here are some tips:
>
> - If you don't understand, don't hesitate to ask. A misunderstanding could cost a life.
>
> - If the person is speaking too quickly, immediately ask him/her to slow down
>
> - As the person is speaking, repeat what is being said. The person will soon realize if you are not understanding.
>
> - Make the excuse that the line is bad and ask the person to speak a bit louder. He/She will usually speak slower as well.

---

d Role-play the following telephone calls.

1 **Student A:** Doctor. Check availability of beds in Observation Ward.*
Student B: Chief Nurse on Observation Ward. Not immediately. In one hour.

2 **Student A:** Senior Nurse. You are short-staffed.* Phone personnel department to request substitute nurse.
Student B: Personnel Assistant. None available until afternoon shift.*

3 **Student A:** Nurse. Order unmatched * blood from blood bank.
Student B: Blood bank orderly.* Where? When? How much?

4 **Student A:** Doctor. Phone pharmacy to check on dose* of a drug. Ask for alternative drug.
Student B: Pharmacist. Give doctor dose. Suggest alternative.

Lesson 2

He'll be fine, Mr Slenkovich

a Read the conversation between a nurse and Wayne's father. Complete the sentences with verbs in the correct tense. Then listen and check your answers.

CD
T-10

Nurse: It's Mr. Slenkovich, Wayne's father, isn't it?

Mr. Slenkovich: That's right. What happened to Wayne? Is he all right?

Nurse: He'll be fine, Mr. Slenkovich. But first things first. It seems that Wayne (1) _____ (finish) work at 8 o'clock in the evening and (2) _____ (just leave) the store when two men (3) _____ (attack) him.

Mr. Slenkovich: (4) _____ (already go) to the bank with the money from the store?

Nurse: I'm really not sure. Anyway, some people (5) _____ (see) the assault and called an ambulance. The paramedics checked Wayne over, put on a neck brace, and brought him in.

Mr. Slenkovich: Did they get the guys who attacked him?

Nurse: I don't know but the police (6) _____ (already speak) to Wayne. Dr. Tan examined him when he arrived and sent him to have a scan. He (7) _____ (have) a dislocated jaw, which we put back in place, but there don't seem to be any broken bones. Anyway, we (8) _____ (decide) to keep him in for the night.

Mr. Slenkovich: Why? If he's OK, why can't he come home?

Nurse: Well he (9) _____ (knock out) for about ten minutes after the attack and the doctor thinks it best to keep an eye on him.

Mr. Slenkovich: Can I see him?

Nurse: Just for a minute. He (10) _____ (need) to rest.

b Find these lay terms in the conversation above. Then match them with the medical terms.

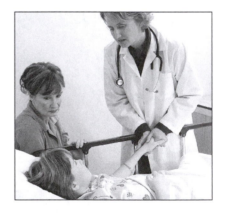

Lay terms		Medical terms
1. _____	keep an eye on him	a. fractures
2. _____	knocked out	b. reposition
3. _____	broken bones	c. unconscious
4. _____	neck collar	d. cervical brace
5. _____	dislocated jaw	e. dislocated mandible
6. _____	put back in place	f. place him under observation

c Role-play the following situations. Use lay terms to explain the cases.

Case 1
Student A: Nurse. Explain case to mother.
Student B: Mother.
James Fox, 6 years old, hit in face by swing at school. Teacher drove him to hospital. One tooth knocked out and retrieved*, one broken.
Missing tooth replaced and splinted*.
Temporary crown* put on broken tooth.
No other injuries besides teeth.

Case 2
Student A: Wife
Student B: Nurse. Explain case to wife.
Art Halamka, 45, chest pain at work. Brought to ER by colleague. Febrile, ECG shows generalized ST segment elevation and there is some pericardial fluid around the heart as shown by echo. The cardiologist diagnosed pericarditis* and is going to drain the fluid.

d Read the discharge instruction guidelines below. Then listen to the nurse giving discharge instructions to Wayne and Mr. Slenkovich. Check ✓ the points she covers.

> **Discharge Instruction Guidelines**
> Make sure patient (or caregiver) knows:
>
> ☐ the name of the doctor who treated him/her.
>
> ☐ the diagnosis.
>
> ☐ dose and possible side effects of medication or treatment.
>
> ☐ precautions to be taken, e.g., no driving, complete rest for two weeks.
>
> ☐ what to do if the condition fails to improve or worsens.
>
> ☐ date and time of follow-up (if any).

e Read the jumbled conversation and number the lines in the correct order. Then practice the conversation with a partner.

☐ **Patient:** 23! Gee! When do they come out?

7 **Nurse:** OK, that's everything finished. You can go home now.

☐ **Nurse:** Erm, let me see . . . 23.

☐ **Patient:** No. I think that's all clear.

☐ **Nurse:** Come back in a week and we'll take them out. It's a bit red now around the cut but that should go away in a day or two. If it doesn't, or if the cut starts to hurt or bleed, then come back right away. OK?

☐ **Patient:** Thanks, nurse. How many stitches* did they put in?

☐ **Nurse:** Yes. You don't need an appointment but it's quieter in the morning. OK, and one more thing, Doctor Byrne wants you to take these pills. Take three a day for six days. They may make you feel a bit drowsy*, so you're not allowed to drive.

☐ **Patient:** Sure. Should I come back here?

☐ **Patient:** No chance of that! My car will be in the body shop for a few weeks, I'm sure.

☐ **Nurse:** OK. Any more questions?

f Role-play giving discharge instructions to the relatives in the cases from exercise **c**.

Case 1

Student A: Nurse.
Student B: Mother
Discharge instructions
Antibiotics, three times a day for a week. Soft food only. Return to dental department in one week. Speak to school about safety of swings.

Case 2

Student A: Wife
Student B: Nurse
Discharge instructions
Colchicine. One pill, twice a day. Report immediately to doctor if there is diarrhea, nausea, vomiting, or stomach pain. Warn that 15 - 30% of patients have recurrences of pericarditis. It can take up to three months for a full recovery. Check-up in cardiology in two weeks.

Lesson 3

Has he ever fainted before

 a Robert is attending a patient, Mr. Legrange. Read the notes and then write the questions you think Robert asked the patient's wife.

➕ Medicall

Patient: ...Chuck Legrange... **Age:** .54.................

CHIEF COMPLAINT: ..Collapsed at home. Semi-conscious on arrival. Confused.

Vital signs: ..BP...80/50. **Respiration rate:** ..30..... **Pulse:** .....90... **Temperature:** .37.1°C.

TRIAGE STATUS: ...Category..I.

..................1..No..previous..history..of..syncope*...

..................2..Hypotensive..medication...

..................3..Had..just..eaten..seafood...

..................4..No..known..allergies..

..................5..No..history..of..trauma...

PHYSICAL ...Patient..is..in..respiratory..distress...He..is..drowsy*..and..pale,..but......
..awakens..when..you..talk..to..him...He..has..generalized..urticaria*...He..has..no.....
..conjunctival*..edema*...His..lips..and..tongue..are..not..swollen*...His..voice....
..sounds..normal...Heart..tachycardic..without..murmurs*...His..lung..examination...
..shows..mild..wheezing*..and..fair..aeration*..with..minimal..retractions*...His.....
..abdomen..is..soft..and..non-tender...*..Face..is..moderately..pale.

---

1. _____ *Has Mr. Legrange had fainting attacks like this before?* _____
2. _____
3. _____
4. _____
5. _____

b Listen to the conversation between Robert and Mrs. Legrange and check your answers.

CD
T-12

c Match the columns.

1. _____ I had just finished dinner	a. that the nurse noticed that she had given him the wrong dose.
2. _____ It was only after the patient became unconscious,	b. when I got this pain in my stomach.
3. _____ The post mortem* indicated	c. Kim had spent almost two years in hospital.
4. _____ By the time she was only four years old,	d. until the patient had already been discharged.
5. _____ The foreign object in the trachea was not noticed	e. that the patient had died from gunshot wounds.

d Robert suspects Mr. Legrange has had a severe allergic reaction to the seafood or the seafood was poisonous. Read the following articles and answer the questions.

Anaphylactic shock

Anaphylactic shock is a severe allergic response by the body to a foreign substance (allergen).

On first contact with the allergen, there is no allergic reaction but the body produces antigen-specific immunoglobulin E (IgE). On subsequent contact, the allergen binds* with the IgE and produces a cascade* of mediators* which include histamine, leukotriene C4, prostaglandin D2, and tryptase. These mediators produce the symptoms of anaphylactic shock.

The most common allergens are drugs (penicillin), intravenous radiocontrast media, stings and certain types of food (shellfish, peanuts).

Symptoms and Signs
Skin: Urticaria,* redness, swelling* of the face, eyelids, lips, tongue, throat, hands and feet.
Respiratory: Difficulty in breathing caused by swelling or spasm of the airway.
Cardiovascular: Hypotension, tachycardia leading to syncope.

Gastrointestinal: Difficulty swallowing, nausea, vomiting diarrhea, abdominal cramping.*
General: Weakness, confusion.

Treatment
The first priority is ABC: Airway, Breathing and Cardiac.

Intubation* may be difficult due to edema* in which case oxygen should be given through bag/valve/mask ventilation. If this does not work then a standard cricothyrotomy* is an option.

It may be necessary in patients with hypotension to start large volume intravenous fluid resuscitation to help restore circulation.

Epinephrine is the drug of choice for severe allergic reactions. It works in two ways: by constricting* the blood vessels, which increases blood pressure, and by widening the airway* to help breathing. Antihistamines are also used as an adjunct.

It is advisable to keep patients under observation for 12 hours.

Scombroid Toxicity

Scombroid toxicity is caused by eating fish which is not fresh. Members of the Scombroidea family which typically have dark meat, e.g., tuna and mackerel, are usually responsible.

Bacteria in the muscles of the fish convert the amino acid histidine into histamine. Histamine is normally present in fish at levels of around .1mg/100g. However levels of 20 - 50 mg/100g are found in fish and cause scombroid toxicity. It is important to note that histamine does not break down when heated.

Symptoms and Signs
Skin: Flushing*, urticarial rash*, swelling of face or tongue, sweating.

Cardiovascular: Tachycardia, hypotension or hypertension.
Gastrointestinal: Nausea, vomiting, diarrhea.
Respiratory: Respiratory distress.
General: Headache, dizziness.

Treatment
The cause of the problem is histamine and so antihistamines such as diphenhydramine are used. Epinephrine is effective but is not usually necessary because there is no full cascade of mediators.

Prognosis
Scombroid toxicity is not life-threatening and patients usually make a full recovery within a few hours.

1. Is it possible to get anaphylactic shock on first contact with an allergen? Give reasons.

2. Would cooking the fish prevent scombroid toxicity? Give reasons.

3. Why are the symptoms of anaphylactic shock and scombroid toxicity very similar?

4. From the information you have, which do you think is the most likely diagnosis for Mr. Legrange. Give reasons.

Lesson 4
I'd like to ask you a few questions

Jenny: So Robert, how's it going?

Robert: Things move quickly around here, don't they? What have we next?

Jenny: A two-year-old child who is wheezing* and having problems breathing.
Here's the Medical Screening Exam. I'd like you to take a look first.

MEDICAL SCREENING EXAM

Patient: ..Louise. Tolan......................   Age: ...2. yrs...........

CHIEF COMPLAINT: ..Difficulty. in. breathing,. wheezing..

BP: ..120/80......................   Respiration Rate: ..80bpm............

Pulse Rate: ...110.............   Temperature: ..38..5°C................

TRIAGE STATUS: ..Category. III................

---

a   If you were Robert, what questions would you ask this patient's parents?
Use the summaries of the illnesses opposite to help you.

_____

_____

_____

_____

_____

_____

_____

b   Listen and write the questions Robert actually does ask. Compare his questions
with your own.

CD
T-13

c   At this stage, what diagnosis would you make? Use the following expressions.

IMPOSSIBLE ⟶ **CERTAIN**

It can't be   It is unlikely to be   It could / might / may be   It's likely to be   It must be

d   Your teacher will tell you what
Robert found when he examined
the patient and also give you
some lab results. What
diagnosis would you make now?

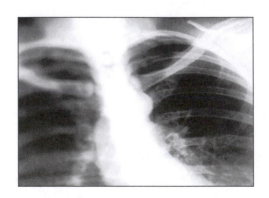

Symptoms and Signs

1. Asthma

✓ Wheezing, cough, breathless during rest, infants are not interested in feeding, sit upright, older children talk in words (not sentences), agitated.
✓ Attacks usually take place at night.
✓ Respiration rate: 30 breaths per minute.
✓ Heart rate: 120 beats per minute.
✓ Retractions.*

2. Cystic fibrosis

Wheezing, cough often followed by vomiting.
Often a history of recurring infections and pneumonia.
Family history.
Lips and fingernails turn blue (cyanosis).
Respiratory distress with retractions.
Increased anterio-posterior diameter of chest.
Clubbing* of fingers.

3. Bronchiolitis*

- Wheezing, fever, poor appetite, dehydration.
- Flared* nostrils.
- Irritability, with difficulty sleeping and signs of fatigue.
- Cyanosis.
- Rapid, shallow breathing (60 to 80 times a minute).
- Rapid heartbeat.

4. Aspiration of foreign body

Episodic cough, difficulty in breathing and wheezing.
Approximately 50% of children have inspiratory stridor★ or expiratory wheezing, with prolongation of the expiratory phase.
Rapid breathing with nasal flaring.★
Intercostal★, subcostal★, and suprasternal★ retractions.
Differences in percussion★ between each side of the chest.
Fever and cyanosis are less common.

5. Croup

- History of mild upper respiratory infection with nasal congestion, sore throat, and loud cough.
- Fever (38 - 39°C).
- Respiratory stridor usually develops at night.
- Inspiratory stridor with nasal flaring,
- Suprasternal and intercostal retractions.
- Lethargy or agitation may be a result of hypoxemia.*
- Rapid heart rate, fast breathing.
- Children may be unable to maintain adequate oral intake resulting in dehydration.
- Cyanosis is a late ominous sign.

Lesson 5

We need to take a sample

a Listen and take notes about the signs and symptoms the patient presents.

CD
T-14

Patient Number: ...26498533...

Name: .Susan..Thorpe..

Address: .17..Oakview..Terrace........ Home phone: ..37489291...........

Occupation: .Bank..clerk...................... Age: .24.........................

Date: 1/12/06........................	c/o* fever, headache................................
Time: 4.30 p.m.....................	T 99.2(o), P 86, R 18, BP 120/80 (L)......
....	....
....	....
....	....
....	....

b Write four other questions that you would like to ask the patient.

1. _____

2. _____

3. _____

4. _____

c Read the conversation and underline the most appropriate word or expression. Compare your answers with those of a partner.

Nurse: Good afternoon, Susan. Has the doctor explained what he is going to do?

Susan: He mentioned a lumbar something.

Nurse: OK. Let me explain. We need to get a sample of (1) a. *CSF** b. *cerebrospinal fluid**

      c. *fluid from your spine to check if you have* (2) a. *a brain infection* b. *meningitis* c. *anything wrong.*

Susan: What! He's gong to put a needle in my brain?

Nurse: No, don't worry. We take the sample from your back.

Susan: Will it hurt?

Nurse: No, we will (3) a. *give you a local anesthetic* b. *inject some lignocaine** c. *numb* your back first.*

Susan: What happens then?

Nurse: The doctor then (4) a. *sucks out* b. *takes out* c. *aspirates some fluid and we send it to the lab. Easy!*

Susan: I hope so.

d Circle the word or expression most appropriate to use with patients. Compare your answers with those of a partner.

1.	2.	3.	4.
a) excise the growth	a) put you to sleep	a) analgesic	a) jab
b) cut the growth out	b) anesthetize you	b) pain killer	b) injection
c) remove the growth	c) put you out	c) pain reliever	c) shot
5.	**6.**	**7.**	**8.**
a) investigate	a) swelling	a) cachexic*	a) intestinal hemorrhage
b) take a look at	b) lump	b) underweight	b) bleeding in your abdomen
c) assess	c) tumor	c) skinny	c) blood loss from your intestines
9.	**10.**	**11.**	**12.**
a) hypertensive medication	a) insert a catheter	a) to produce a stool	a) to go to the bathroom
b) some pills to lower your blood pressure	b) put in a tube	b) to defecate	b) to urinate
c) little yellow pills	c) introduce a catheter	c) to move your bowels	c) to take a pee

e Rewrite the following sentences so that they sound less threatening for a patient.

1. We'll have to perform surgery to cut out the tumor.

    You'll need a small operation to remove the swelling.

2. We need to investigate the possibility that you have cancer.

    _____

3. I am going to put a catheter in your urethra to collect your urine.

    _____

4. The only way I can get this tooth out is to cut away a piece of bone and lever* it out.

    _____

5. We will have to drill a hole in your head to take out the fluid.

    _____

6. I am going to administer a subcutaneous injection into the deltoid muscle.

    _____

 f Think of a situation in your own field that requires careful use of words. Explain it to the class.

Lesson 6

Can I explain the procedure

a Put the sentences below in the correct order to describe the lumbar puncture procedure.

☐ Advance the needle 2 cm until you hear a "pop" sound. This is when the needle passes through the dura.* Then advance the needle 2-3mm, and check for CSF. Continue until CSF is returned. If you hit bone or blood returns, withdraw to the skin and redirect the needle.

☐ Attach the manometer* and measure the pressure.

☐ Remove the manometer and collect three samples (about 1-2 cc each) of the CSF for testing.

☐ Sterilize the puncture site.

☐ Then locate the puncture site. This is between the 4th and 5th lumbar vertebrae. The 4th lumbar vertebra is level with the superior iliac crest.*

☐ Using a 25-gauge needle, inject 1% lidocaine to anesthetize the skin at the puncture site. The needle should be in the midline* and pointing towards the patient's umbilicus.*

☐ When CSF begins to flow, discard the first few drops.

1 Have the patient lie on the edge of the bed, facing away from the operator. The knees should be lifted up to the chest and the neck flexed*. The head should be resting on a pillow and the whole of the spine parallel to the ground. This is to ensure an accurate pressure reading.

b Susan's lab tests are back. Read the following data and the results of Susan's tests and make a diagnosis.

	Normal	Bacterial meningitis	Viral meningitis
CSF Pressure	< 30 mm H2O	Raised	Normal
Color	Clear	Sometimes turbid*	Clear
Cell count	< 5 x 106 /L	Increased	Increased
Differential	Lymphocytes (60-70%) Monocytes (30-50%) Neutrophils (None)	High neutrophil count	High lymphocyte count
Protein	0.15-0.45 g/L	Increased	Normal or slight increase.
CSF / serum glucose ratio*	> 60%	Reduced	Normal or slight increase.
Gram's stain *		Sometimes positive	Negative

Protein: 1.2 g/L
CSF Glucose: 2 .0 mM
Serum glucose: 6.0 mM
Cell count: 200 red blood cells, 200 white blood cells x $\frac{106}{L}$
90% neutrophils
Gram's stain: Negative

C Read the article and answer the questions.

Causes and Treatment of Bacterial Meningitis

Streptococcus pneumonia (pneumococcus)

This is a very common cause of meningitis in the United States. It mainly affects young children and older people but it can infect anyone. In recent years, some types of Streptococcus pneumonia have become resistant to penicillin but fortunately the organism is still susceptible to the third-generation cephalosporins.*

Neisseria meningitiditis (meningococcus)

This organism is highly contagious and is often responsible for mass outbreak in college dormitories and military bases. It often begins with an upper respiratory tract infection and then spreads to the brain. Penicillin is the drug of choice but resistant strains* have been reported and these are best treated with ceftriaxone.

Haemophilus influenzae (haemophilus)

This bacterium used to be the most common cause of meningitis but since the introduction of vaccinations, it has become less common. When it is met, third-generation cephalosporins are the treatment of choice.

These three bacteria account for over 80% of meningitis cases. Less common causative agents include *Escherichia coli,* which mainly affects neonates, and *Listeria monocytogenes,* which tends to affect the elderly.

The use of steroids

Recent studies have indicated that when steroids* are used alongside antibiotics, there is a lowering of mortality and other unfavorable outcomes.

It is thought that steroids help by reducing the body's inflammatory reaction to the breakdown products that are produced when the antibiotics kill the bacteria. It is therefore crucial that the steroids are given *before* or *with* the first dose of antibiotics so that they are present in the tissues when the initial inflammatory burst* occurs.

1. According to the article, how many different types of bacteria are responsible for meningitis?

_____

2. Of these bacteria, which do you think are most likely to be responsible for Susan's meningitis?

_____

3. Identifying the specific bacteria takes at least 24 hours and Susan needs treatment urgently. Which antibiotics would you give?

_____

4. Explain why it is important that steroids are given early in the treatment of meningitis.

_____

Team Project

FIRST AID
All health care professionals, and indeed all adults, need to know some basic first aid procedures.

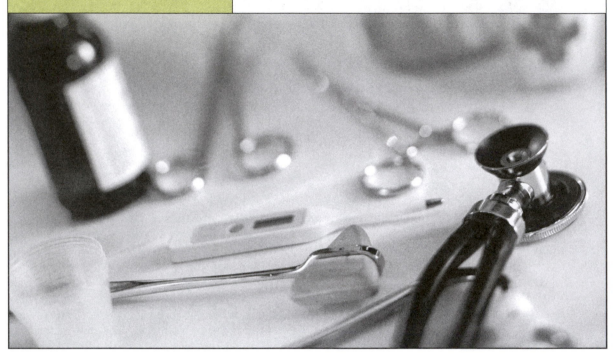

A Research Phase

Work in groups and research first aid for ONE of the following:

- Drug overdose
- Electric shocks
- Choking
- Fainting

- Broken bones
- Nosebleeds
- Sports injuries
- Unconsciousness

Or you can choose another topic that is relevant to your field.

You should find information on:
- How to recognize / diagnose the condition.
- What to do.
- What not to do.
- What preventative measures, if any, could be taken.

B Presentation Phase

- Present your findings to the class.
- Use pictures or posters / charts to make your presentations more interesting.

> **Useful Key Words**
>
> first aid
> emergency treatment

Unit 3

Breaking bad news

Can you describe the pain

a Brainstorm as many words as possible related to pain.

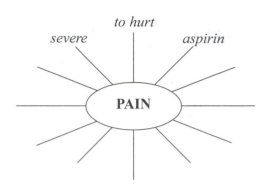

```
         to hurt
severe              aspirin


          PAIN

```

b Match the columns.

Features of pain	Main questions	Follow-up questions
1. _g I VI VIII_ Location	a. How long does the pain last?	I. Is it near the surface of your body or deep inside?
2. _____ Triggering* factors	b. Does anything bring the pain on?	II. Does a hot-water bottle or ice pack help?
3. _____ Duration	c. Can you describe the pain?	III. Do you feel better standing, sitting, or lying down, for example?
4. _____ Intensity & character	d. Does anything make the pain worse?	IV. Does it hurt all the time?
5. _____ Onset	e. Have you had a pain like this before?	V. Have you had to stop doing certain activities like walking or climbing stairs because of the pain?
6. _____ Timing	f. When do you get the pain?	VI. Does it start in one place and spread?
7. _____ Alleviating* factors	g. Where is the pain?	VII. Does the pain make it difficult for you to concentrate?
8. _____ Aggravating* factors	h. When did the pain start?	VIII. Is it in one part of your body or in more than one place?
9. _____ Previous occurrence	i. Does anything make the pain better?	IX. Does it come on slowly or quickly?

c Write the words in the box in the correct columns.

aching*	pressing*	unbearable*	hot	slight*	excruciating*	tingling*
stabbing	blunt*	throbbing*	annoying	intense	dull*	

Intensity of pain		Character of pain
Severe	**Mild**	

d Unscramble and complete the following sentences, using the word order 1) Intensity, 2) Character, 3) Location, 4) Duration.

1. aching / in his back / for three weeks / dull / pain

   The patient has a dull, aching pain in his back that has lasted for three weeks.

2. in his chest / since yesterday / stabbing / intense / pain

   _____

3. excruciating / for two days / headache / throbbing

   _____

4. in her fingers / mild / for 2 months / cramp

   _____

5. earache / unbearable / throbbing / for 3 days

   _____

e Work with a partner and practice dialogues using the sentences from exercise **d**. Use the main questions and follow-up questions from exercise **b** to continue the dialogues. Example:

A: Can you tell me about the pain?
B: I have had a dull, aching pain in my back that has lasted for 3 weeks.
A: Does it hurt all the time?
B: No, it comes on later in the day.
A: Does anything make it better?
B: Yes, lying down or taking a hot bath.

Lesson 2

It's how you say it

a You will hear the following sentences said twice; once with an "accusing" tone of voice and once with a "supporting" tone of voice. Write which tone is used <u>first</u> (1) and which tone is used <u>second</u> (2).

CD T-15

	Accusing tone	Supporting tone
1. *You should have called me.*	2	1
2. Why didn't you come sooner?		
3. Sorry, what did you say?		
4. Did you understand what I said?		
5. How many times have you been here?		
6. Why didn't you finish the treatment?		

● **Communication Tip**

The old saying, "It's not *what* you say, it's *how* you say it" is especially true in the medical field. A small change in a health care provider's intonation can completely change a patient's attitude and cooperation.

b Listen to the recording again and repeat the sentences with the supporting tone.

CD T-16

c Read these sentences to each other using a supporting tone. Then listen to check your intonation.

CD T-17

Student A reads to Student B	Student B reads to Student A
1. Why didn't you let me know sooner?	2. Are you telling me everything?
3. Sorry, can you say that again?	4. I don't think I need to see you again.
5. What do you mean by that?	6. And don't forget to bring the urine sample.
7. I don't think there's anything wrong with you.	8. Why didn't you call me?

d Listen to the patient interview and decide who has a more supporting tone, Dr. Murray or Robert.

CD T-18

● **Communication Tip**

A new syndrome, known as the "door knob syndrome" has been described in the literature. This takes place after a doctor-patient interview when the patient reaches the office door and says to the doctor, "Oh doctor, there is something else."

The remedy is simple. The doctor simply has to say "Is that everything?" at the end of the interview to allow the patient to bring up anything else that is worrying him or her.

e Listen again and fill in the missing notes.

CD
T-19

Name: *John Bloom*   **Age:** *36*   **Occupation:** *Engineer*
Chief Complaint: *"bad back"*

1. *Onset:* _____
2. *Location:* _____
3. *Intensity and character:* *like a cramp, seems like the muscles are all stiff*
4. *Duration:* _____
5. *Timing:* *bad in the morning* _____
6. *Triggering factors:* _____
7. *Alleviating factors:* *taking a nap* _____
8. *Aggravating factors:* _____
9. *Previous occurrences:* _____
10. *Family history:* *none known* _____
11. *Social History:* _____

 f Role-play taking a history of pain of the following cases. Student **A** is the doctor and Student **B**, the patient. Reverse roles after each card.

Card 1

You have had an intense sharp* pain in the right side of your chest for ten days. It hurts a lot when you breathe. The pain starts on the tip of your right shoulder and spreads down to your ribs. The pain is much worse if you move around and you have to lie still all the time. When you try to sit up, it is very painful.

Card 2

You have a severe, shooting* pain that travels down the back of your left leg to your ankle. It sometimes starts when you are sitting doing nothing, but at other times if you sneeze or cough, the pain begins. You also have a tingling, burning feeling most of the time in your leg. The pain gets better if you lift your knees up to your chest. It started a month ago and has been getting worse.

Card 3

You are getting intense pain on your right cheek. It is excruciatingly painful. It starts if you touch any part of your face. Brushing your teeth can also start it off. It lasts just a few seconds but you get attacks many times per day. Nothing seems to make it better.

Card 4

You have been having severe headaches for the last 3 weeks. It starts with a dull ache on the left side of your neck and builds up to a severe, throbbing headache on the left side of your head. Before the pain starts, you start seeing "spots" in front of your eyes and during the headache you cannot tolerate light. It usually lasts for about three hours.

Lesson 3

It's getting you down, isn't it

 a Read the following conversation between Mr. Bloom and a nurse in Radiography. Replace the phrasal verbs in italics with expressions from the box. Then practice the dialogue.

comes	depressing me	discuss this	persevere	tolerate it	discover

Nurse: Morning, Mr. Bloom. Here for your tests?

Mr. Bloom: That's right.

Nurse: And how are you feeling?

Mr. Bloom: Oh, my back's really *getting me down*.
(1) _____

Nurse: If you can just *stick it out* (2) _____
a bit longer, I'm sure they'll *find out* (3) _____
_____ what's wrong.

Mr. Bloom: I hope so. I don't think I can *put up with it*
(4) _____ any longer.

Nurse: OK, well you can *talk this over* (5) _____
_____ with the doctor.

Mr. Bloom: Yes, when he *shows up*. (6) _____

Nurse: He's very busy, but he should be here in a
short while.

> **● Communication Tip**
>
> Phrasal verbs, e.g. *to put up with*, are used in informal, non-technical speech. Their equivalents, e.g. *to tolerate*, tend to be more formal. When speaking with patients, it is better to use phrasal verbs.

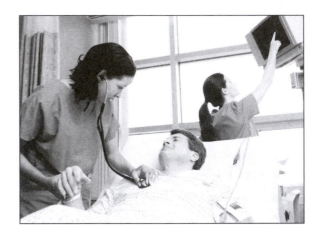

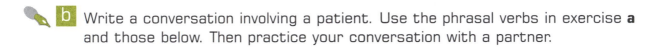 **b** Write a conversation involving a patient. Use the phrasal verbs in exercise **a** and those below. Then practice your conversation with a partner.

Phrasal verb	Definition	Example
get over	to recover	It's not a serious illness. You'll *get over* it in a couple of weeks.
give up/in	to abandon hope, to surrender	You fought so hard, don't *give up / in* now.
come down with	to start an illness	She got flu first and then the whole family *came down with* it.
go through with	to proceed in spite of fears	I have decided to *go through with* the operation.
hold out	not to surrender	It hurts, but I think I can *hold out* for another few days.
keep on	to continue	I know those pills taste terrible but you have to *keep on* taking them.
stick with	to persist, to continue	I know this is taking a long time, but you will just have to *stick with* it.

c Dave, the radiographer, is having problems with his equipment. Read the telephone conversation and fill in the blanks with question tags.

Dave: Hi, Chuck. It's Dave. We are having a problem with the XL45 again. The films are coming out clear.

Chuck: Oh no, and I'm really busy at the moment. Can we just run over a few things on the phone?

Dave: Sure thing. Shoot.

Chuck: First, it's plugged in, (1) _isn't it_ ?

Dave: Give me a break. Of course it is.

Chuck: You didn't leave the collimator shutters closed, (2) _____ ?

Dave: No, I don't think so.

Chuck: You haven't been playing with the gain control, (3) _____ ?

Dave: Never touched it.

Chuck: What about the footswitch? You are keeping your foot on it all the time, (4) _____ ?

Dave: Sure.

Chuck: OK, well it looks like I'll have to come over. You'll still be there this afternoon, (5) _____ ?

Dave: I finish at 10:00 today. So if you can come as soon as possible, I would appreciate it.

Chuck: I'll do my best. See you later.

CD T-20

d You will hear the following question tags said twice, once as a confirmation and once as a question. Write which is said **first** (1) and which is said **second** (2).

	Confirmation	Question
1. *Mr. Bloom's next, isn't he?*	1	2
2. You've got Mr. Bloom's notes, haven't you?	_____	_____
3. You're here for a chest X-ray, aren't you?	_____	_____
4. This isn't going to hurt, is it?	_____	_____
5. I can leave now, can't I?	_____	_____

CD T-21

e Listen to the recording again and repeat the sentences.

---

f Write five sentences using question tags. Read your sentences to a partner using either a confirmation or a question tone. Your partner must identify which tone you are using.

1. _____

2. _____

3. _____

4. _____

5. _____

Lesson 4

We need a psychiatric evaluation

a Work in pairs. Try to recall the details of Mr. Bloom's case from memory.

b Read and listen to the conversation between Dr. Murray and Robert. Underline the verb forms in the passive voice. Then practice the conversation.

CD
T-22

Dr. Murray: So, Robert, let's go over Mr. Bloom's case. Can you review it for me?

Robert: Sure. The patient presented on February 4 this year complaining of lower back pain. There was no history of trauma. Analgesics were prescribed and the patient was advised to avoid strenuous work and heavy lifting.

Dr. Murray: Go on.

Robert: The patient was seen again on April 6 complaining that he was still in pain and that the condition was worse. He also complained of depression. The patient was referred for radiography.

Dr. Murray: OK. Let's have a look at the radiograph. What do you think?

Robert: Let me see. Well, it looks fine to me.

Dr. Murray: To me, too. So what do you suggest?

Robert: Well, I think he should be referred for a psychological evaluation at this point. Maybe the back pain is psychosomatic. After all, he seems to be rather depressed.

Dr. Murray: All right. That might be valuable but I also think he ought to be referred to a neurologist.

c Write the verbs in the passive voice.

Case 1

The patient (involve) **(1)** _was involved_ in a road traffic accident and **(2)** (take) _____ to Emergency where he **(3)** (examine) _____ by Dr. Singh. Radiographs **(4)** (request) _____ _____ and a compound fracture of the femur **(5)** (find) _____. He **(6)** (admit) _____ and **(7)** (take) _____ to the operating room where the fracture **(8)** (stabilize) _____ by Dr. Massoud.

Case 2

The patient **(1)** (see) _____ by Dr Helingbaum and a mucocele * **(2)** (find) _____ on the lower lip. The cyst **(3)** (excise) _____ under local anesthetic and the patient **(4)** (instruct) _____ to return the following week when the sutures **(5)** (remove) _____.

Case 3

The patient, a 72-year-old male, **(1)** (admit) _____ on Sunday evening in acute respiratory distress. On examination, the patient **(2)** (find) _____ to be cyanotic* and with blood pressure of 80/55. On chest auscultation,* crackles **(3)** (hear) _____. The patient **(4)** (sedate) _____ and **(5)** (place) _____ on a ventilator. He is responding well to treatment.

d Role-play explaining the cases in exercise **c** to a relative or colleague using the active voice and less formal language.

Example:

Case 1

Your son was in a car accident so they brought him here. Dr. Singh checked him and found a very bad fracture of his thigh bone. So, they took him to the operating room and Dr. Massoud set the fracture.

> **● Communication Tip**
>
> The passive voice is more formal than the active voice and is often used when professionals are speaking or writing to other professionals. It is more appropriate to use the active voice with patients, patients' relatives and close colleagues.

 e In your notebook, write another case history in the passive voice and then practice explaining it in less formal language to your group.

f Read the referral letter and underline the passives.

Ashville Medical Center
Primary Care Unit

To: Dr. Ruth Fendwick, Department of Psychiatry

Dear Ruth

I would be grateful if you would do a psychiatric evaluation of the following patient: James Bloom, a 34-year-old engineer, presented 3 months ago complaining of a stiff, painful back and depression. A thorough physical examination <u>was performed</u>, but no cause of the symptoms was found. Radiographs were taken but no abnormalities were reported.

I have been unable to detect any physical cause of the problem but diazepam was prescribed and the patient reported an improvement.

I would therefore like to investigate the possibility of the symptoms being of psychiatric origin.

Yours sincerely

Bruce Murray MD

 g Write another referral letter to a psychiatrist for the following case.

Selena Hislop, Travel Agent, 56 yrs.
Presenting complaint: halitosis*
Physical Examination: At time of exam, no halitosis detected. No apparent medical or dental cause.

Lesson 5

It might be multiple sclerosis

a Listen and fill in the table as Robert reports the results of his literature review.

CD
T-23

Illness	Main symptoms	Mental status
Chronic generalized tetanus	■ Lockjaw* (75% of cases) ■ Stiffness of (1) _____	(2) _____
Stiff Person Syndrome	■ Painful muscular spasms* in back and (3) _____ limbs. ■ Spasms occur with strong emotional stimulus, e.g., surprise, anger. ■ Spasms (5) _____ during sleep.	(4) _____ in most patients.
Isaac's Syndrome	■ Progressive stiffness and spasms. ■ Rippling* movement of muscles. ■ Spasms (6) _____ during sleep.	Normal
Multiple Sclerosis	■ Painful muscle spasms. ■ Parasthesia or (7) _____ ■ Fatigue	Depression in (8) _____ patients.

b In groups, discuss which is the most likely diagnosis for Mr. Bloom. Use the following expressions:

IMPOSSIBLE ➜ CERTAIN

| It can't be | It is unlikely to be | It could / might / may be | It's likely to be | It must be |

c Read the neurologist's report on Mr. Bloom. Number the paragraphs in the correct order.

Ashville Medical Center
Department of Neurology

AMC
Department of Neurology

Re: James Bloom

☐ Thank you for referring the above patient.

☐ My diagnosis, therefore, is that the patient is suffering from Stiff Person Syndrome.

☐ The patient complains of painful spasms in the back and shoulders, which relapse when sleeping. Associated depression was also reported. The patient denies any sensory neuropathy.*

☐ I would be happy to arrange treatment and follow-up in the department.

☐ On examination, I noted that the patient had an exaggerated upright and stiff posture* and there was a marked startle response.* I arranged a GAD antibody test* and the results were positive.

☑ Dear Bruce

Yours sincerely
Gurdev
Dr. Gurdev Chandaraseka MD

d Discuss the differential diagnosis of the following patient.
What follow-up questions would you like to ask? What tests would be useful?

56-year-old, obese male presented with left-sided chest pain, which began after working in the garden. Had eaten lunch one hour earlier. Nausea and vomiting. Similar episodes for one week. Last episode after eating dinner yesterday. Pain goes away when lying down.

Illness	Main symptoms
Pericarditis	Sharp retrosternal* chest pain, which is often improved by sitting forward. Worse with inspiration and associated shortness of breath, palpitations, shoulder discomfort, and cough. Change of posture and breathing influence the pain.
Myocardial infarction	Continuous, pressing, retrosternal chest pain. Lasts about 20 minutes. Possibly radiating to the arms (usually to the left arm), back, neck, or the lower jaw. Intensity does not alter. Breathing or changing posture does not influence the severity of the pain. Episodes of pain are related to activity; relief with rest.
Pleuritis	Nausea and vomiting are sometimes the main symptoms. Sometimes hypotension, presenting as dizziness or fainting. A localized stabbing pain when breathing. Associated with recent or present respiratory illness. Fever, malaise. Aggravated by coughing and deep breathing.
Gastroesophageal reflux (hiatal hernia)	Burning or pressing pain in the middle of the chest. Associated with eating. May be triggered by exercise. Nausea. Worse lying down.
Pulmonary embolism	Central stabbing chest pain; also may be burning, aching or dull, heavy sensation. Rapid breathing. Tachycardia. Pain is often not severe although onset is sudden. May be worsened by breathing deeply, coughing, eating, or bending.

Lesson 6

I'm afraid to say that . . .

a Read the article on Stiff Person Syndrome and write the verbs in parentheses in the passive voice. Then answer the questions in your notebook.

STIFF PERSON SYNDROME

Stiff Person Syndrome (SPS) (first describe) (1) _____*was first described*_____ in 1956 by Moersch and Woltmann. It (think) (2) _____ to be an auto immune disease and it (associate) (3) _____ with other auto immune diseases like diabetes and hyperthyroidism.

High levels of an antibody to the enzyme GAD (find) (4) _____ in many patients. GAD (involve) (5) _____ in the production of GABA, a neurotransmitter. The functions of GABA (not clearly understand) (6) _____ but it appears to be involved in the suppression* of voluntary muscle stimulation. If GAD levels (lower) (7) _____ significantly, then the availability of GABA (decrease) (8) _____ and muscles become continuously stimulated by the motor neurons. GABA (also involve) (9) _____ in the suppression of anxiety.

SPS (characterize) (10) _____ by muscle spasms in the back and shoulders. The spasms (precipitate*) (11) _____ by emotional distress and they (often relieve) (12) _____ _____ with sleep. Depression and anxiety (often report) (13) _____ by patients. If the patient presents at an early stage, few objective findings may be found initially. Unfortunately, because of the lack of clear symptoms and apparent strong psychological components, these patients (often label) (14) _____ as psychogenic and effective treatment (often delay) (15) _____.

SPS (usually treat) (16) _____ by benzodiazepines but recent research has indicated that intravenous immunoglobulin is effective in some cases. Physiotherapy (need) (17) _____ by nearly all patients.

The prognosis of the disease is variable. Some patients respond well to treatment and only have episodes of stiffness. Other patients become severely physically and mentally handicapped.

1. According to the article, do all patients with SPS have diabetes? Explain your answer.

_____

2. How do high levels of antibodies to GAD cause muscle spasms?

_____

3. What makes the muscle spasms worse and what makes them better?

_____

4. Which parts of the article would you not tell to a patient? Why?

_____

5. Stiff Person Syndrome was originally called Stiff Man Syndrome. Why do you think the name was changed?

_____

b Decide whether the following ways of breaking bad news are *direct* or *indirect*. Then compare your answers with those of another student.

Direct	Indirect	
☐	☐	a. Listen, I've got some bad news for you.
☐	☐	b. I'm afraid to say that your tests are not very encouraging.
☐	☐	c. OK, your tests are back and it seems as though we may have a more serious problem than we first thought.
☐	☐	d. I'm going to be frank with you. It seems as though you have a terminal illness.
☐	☐	e. Well, your scans are back and it appears you have a rather suspicious growth.
☐	☐	f. I am about 90% certain that when we do the biopsy, we are going to find cancer.

 c Role-play the following situation.

Student A: Doctor
Task: First, break the news that Mr. Bloom has SPS. Think carefully about how you will do this. Then describe the condition to the patient and answer his questions.
Student B: Mr. Bloom
Task: Before the role play, prepare some questions that you would like to ask the doctor about the diagnosis, its causes, treatment, progress, prognosis, etc.

 d Role-play explaining the following situations to patients or superiors. Change roles after each situation.

1. Dentist: When extracting a lower premolar, you cut the mental nerve (the nerve that supplies the lower lip). Sometimes the loss of sensation is permanent, sometimes there is a feeling of parasthesia ("pins and needles"), and sometimes there is a full recovery.

2. Nurse: You gave the wrong dose of medication to a patient. Break the news to the doctor.

> ● **Communication Tip**
>
> In some societies, direct eye contact is seen as being rude. However, in the United States, it indicates concern and interest on the part of both speaker and listener.

3. Radiographer: A patient was referred with a suspected fracture of the cranium for an emergency X-ray and you forgot to put the slide in the X-ray machine. Explain to the radiologist.

4. General Practitioner: You referred a 78-year-old patient to a cancer specialist, and the results indicate that the patient has a large, aggressive, malignant tumor in the lung and also has bone metastases.* Surgery is impossible and chemotherapy is unlikely to work.

e Work with a partner. Each of you should think of a situation where you, as health care professionals, have had to break bad news, either to a patient or a superior. Role-play the situations.

RARE DISEASES

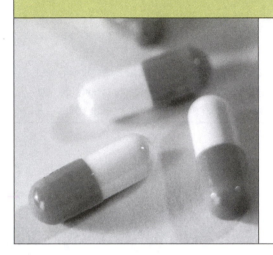

In the United States, a rare disease is defined as a disease that affects less than 200,000 people. However, there are some diseases that affect just a handful of people.

Drug companies are very reluctant to spend money researching new drugs for rare diseases because sales would be so low they would never get their investment back again.

A Research Phase

Work in groups and research ONE of the following rare diseases:

Jumping Frenchmen of Maine
Sudden Infant Death Syndrome
Jamaican Vomiting Sickness
Q fever
OR
Another rare disease relevant to your field

You will need to find information on:

Useful Key Words
rare diseases
orphan diseases

- cause

- symptoms

- physical signs

- typical patient (age, gender, occupation, relevant social background)

- investigations

- treatment

- prognosis

B Presentation Phase

- Present your findings to the class.

- Use pictures or posters/charts.

Unit 4

Calling in the Stroke Team

She can hardly speak

a Robert is now working with Dr. Oliveira. Dr. Oliveira is interviewing a patient and her husband. Write her questions.

Dr. Oliveira: Now, what is the problem, Mrs. Marshall?

Mr. Marshall: Sorry, doctor, but she seems to be having problems talking. *I can't hardly* understand her.

Dr. Oliveira: (1) _____

Mr. Marshall: About *two hours back, I guess.* Around nine o'clock.

Dr. Oliveira: (2) _____

Mr. Marshall: We were working *out back* and she said that her chest was starting *to pain* her again.

Dr. Oliveira: (3) _____

Mr. Marshall: *You bet* she's had chest pains before. She was in hospital two weeks ago, over in California when we were seeing our son.

Dr. Oliveira: (4) _____

Mr. Marshall: Well, she sat down and took a little rest. She said she was feeling better.

Dr. Oliveira: (5) _____

Mr. Marshall: Well, then I noticed that she was speaking kind of funny. And she couldn't walk *real good*. Her hand and arm were funny as well.

Dr. Oliveira: (6) _____

Mr. Marshall: That would be her right side.

Dr. Oliveira: (7) _____

Mr. Marshall: Yes, she is taking some little white pills for her high blood pressure.

Dr. Oliveira: (8) _____

Mr. Marshall: Yes, I brought them with me. Here they are.

Dr. Oliveira: Yes, you're right. They're metoprobonol, it's a B blocker. OK, it's time to have a look at your wife.

b Mr. Marshall uses some colloquial American expressions. Write their formal equivalents in the right-hand column.

Colloquial American English	Formal English
1. *I can't hardly*	*I can hardly*
2. two hours back	
3. I guess	
4. out back	
5. to pain	
6. you bet	
7. real good	

c Fill in as many gaps as possible using the information from the consultation on the previous page.

Last name: (1) _Marshall_	**First name:** (2) _____	**Age:** (3) _____

Occupation: (4) _____   **Marital status:** (5) _____

Chief complaint:
Chest pain starting (6) _____ ago. Shortly after she developed numbness* and weakness
on (7) _____ side. Mild dysarthria.

Blood pressure:	**Heart rate:**	**Respiratory rate:**	**Temperature:**
(8) _____	(9) _____	(10) _____	(11) _____

Past medical history:
Patient treated for "(12) _____ " 2/52 ago.
Hypertension.

Social history: No alcohol. Quit smoking sixteen years ago.
Medication: (13) _____

d Dr. Oliveira is calling the head of the Stroke Team. Listen to the call and fill in the rest of the information in the Patient's Medical Record above.

CD
T-24

e Write five questions that you would ask the following patient's relatives.

Case 1: 80-year-old woman, living alone, found unconscious by visiting daughter.

1. _____
2. _____
3. _____
4. _____
5. _____

Case 2: 8-month-old baby, vomiting blood.

1. _____
2. _____
3. _____
4. _____
5. _____

f Role-play taking a history of the two cases in Exercise **d**.

Lesson 2
How many fingers can you see

a Below are the guidelines for <u>some</u> of the NIH (National Institute of Health) Stroke Scale categories. If you were the doctor testing these categories, what instructions and/or explanations would you give Mrs. Marshall? Remember that Mrs. Marshall seems to understand but can't speak.

3 Visual fields
Visual fields of both eyes are examined. In most cases, the physician asks the patient to count fingers in all four quadrants.* Each eye is independently tested. If a patient is unable to respond verbally, the physician should have the patient hold up the number of fingers seen.

OK, Mrs. Marshall, I'm going to check how much you can see. I'm going to hold up some fingers in different places and I want you to hold up the same number of fingers. OK?

4 Facial movement
The patient is examined by looking at the patient's face and noting any spontaneous facial movements. The facial movements in response to commands are also tested. Such commands may include asking the patient to grimace* or smile, to puff out* his/her cheeks, to pucker*, and to close his/her eyes forcefully.

_____
_____
_____
_____

7 Limb ataxia*
The patient is examined for evidence of a unilateral cerebellar lesion.* Limb movement abnormalities related to sensory or motor dysfunction are also detected. Limb ataxia is checked by the finger-to-nose and heel-to-shin* tests. The "normal" side should be checked first. The movements should be well performed, smooth, accurate, and non-clumsy.*

_____
_____
_____

9 Sensory
The patient is examined with a pin in the proximal* portions of all four limbs and asked how the stimulus feels. The patient's eyes do not need to be closed. The patient is asked if the stimulus is sharp or dull and if there is any asymmetry* between the right and left sides.

_____
_____
_____

b Fill in the gaps with words from the box.

normal	therapy	onset	diagnosis	administered	effective

A computed tomography, or CT, scan is essential when a stroke is suspected for the following reason.

The main (1) _____ for strokes is the use of thrombolytic agents. These would be dangerous if (2) _____ to patients with hemorrhagic* strokes and so it is important to have a clear (3) _____ of an ischemic* stroke before thrombolytics are administered.

However, the first signs of intra-cranial ischemia appear on CT scans about five to six hours after the (4) _____ of symptoms and thrombolytics are only (5) _____ if administered in the first three hours of the crisis. Therefore, a (6) _____ CT scan of the brain is required for the administration of thrombolytics.

 c Read the following text about CT scans. Then role-play explaining the purpose and procedure of a CT scan to Mr. and Mrs. Marshall.

The CT scanner

A CT scanner is basically an X-ray machine that revolves around the patient. Instead of using photographic plates to capture the X-rays, it uses electronic sensors. These sensors convert the X-rays into digital data, which are then sent to a computer. This computer processes the information and produces images of "slices" of the body.

The CT scan has a major advantage over normal radiographs in that it allows the doctor to see soft tissue lesions.* Hence, CT scans are indispensable in the evaluation of cerebro-vascular accidents, or strokes, as all the damage is in the soft tissues.

The following precautions have to be taken:
- It is important that the patient remove all metal or plastic objects (earrings, dentures, glasses, etc.) before the scan.
- It is necessary for all radiology staff and relatives to leave the room. If the patient is anxious about this, then reassure them that they can see the control room and that there is two-way communication between the patient and the staff or relatives. In pediatric cases, a parent may be allowed to stay with the patient but will have to wear a lead apron.*

The procedure is quick and painless. Some patients complain of claustrophobia when they are in the tunnel of the scanner, but as scanners get quicker and quicker, this has become less of a problem.

 d Prepare a short description or explanation of a piece of equipment or procedure that you are familiar with. Present it to the class without mentioning its name. Your classmates have to guess what it is.

Lesson 3

We need to run a few more tests

a Mrs. Marshall is going to have an ECG. Read the text below and fill in the gaps with words from the box.

reassure	generates
surgical	measured
attached	motionless
anterior	diagnose

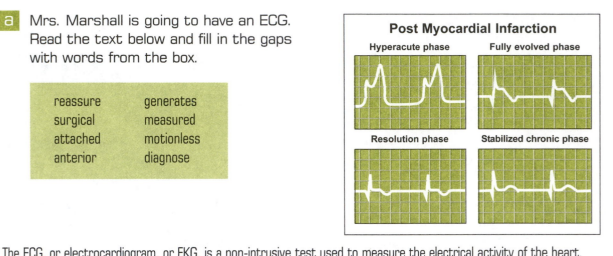

Post Myocardial Infarction

Hyperacute phase	Fully evolved phase
Resolution phase	**Stabilized chronic phase**

The ECG, or electrocardiogram, or EKG, is a non-intrusive test used to measure the electrical activity of the heart. The heart (1) _____ electrical signals that travel through its muscles. However, these signals "leak" out of the heart and pass through the (2) _____ chest wall. This is fortunate because it means that the signals can be easily (3) _____ externally without discomfort to the patient or (4) _____ procedures.
To perform an ECG, sensors are (5) _____ to the arms, legs and chest wall* in very specific places and the ECG machine then automatically produces a number of graphs that the doctor can use to (6) _____ a heart disorder.
Patients are often under the impression that they are going to be electrocuted when they are connected up to the ECG. It may be necessary to (7) _____ them and explain the procedure more clearly.
It is important that the patient remain (8) _____ during the test as any small movements, even trembling or shivering, can affect the results.

b Robert is calling the hospital in California where Mrs. Marshall received treatment ten days ago. Listen and fill in the gaps in his notes.

CD
T-25

PMH
CC: (1) _____ chest pain.
O/E
On admission:
ECG: *ST segment and T wave* (2) _____
Diagnosis: *Acute MI*
Rx: *Morphine 2 mg IV*
(3) _____
Nitroglycerin
Heparin
After 6/24:
ECG: *Reduced ST segment and T wave abnormality.*
Elevated levels of CK-MB myocardial (4) _____
After 24/24:
(5) _____ *subsided. ECG normal. Elevated CK-MB.*
Patient discharged herself after 36/24.

c Work with a partner. Write the full forms of these abbreviations from Exercise **B**.

1. PMH _____
2. O/E _____
3. ECG _____
4. MI _____
5. Rx _____
6. IV _____
7. /24 _____

d Mrs. Marshall needs a drip line.* Put the steps for setting up a drip line in the correct order.

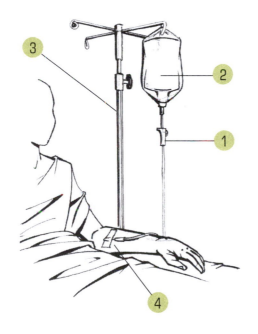

| 1. roller clamp | 3. IV stand |
| 2. IV solution bag | 4. catheter |

☐ *1* Collect all the equipment you will need.

☐ Open the roller clamp to allow the correct flow of fluid.

☐ Attach tubing to IV bag, open roller clamp, and fill tubing with fluid, close clamp.

☐ Set up the IV stand.

☐ Secure the catheter to the skin with adhesive tape.

☐ Apply a tourniquet* around the patient's arm, 10 cm above the elbow.

☐ Select a vein, cleanse with alcohol, insert the needle rapidly and smoothly through the skin into the vein.

☐ Fill in the patient's details on the label, attach it to the IV solution bag and hang the bag on the IV stand.

☐ Wash your hands and put on gloves.

☐ When blood appears, attach the catheter to the tubing.

e Work in pairs. Role-play the following situations.

1. Student A explains the purpose and procedure of an ECG to student B.
2. Student B explains the purpose and procedure of putting up a drip line to student A.

Lesson 4
What medication would you prescribe

 a Find a partner and role-play the following situation.

Student A: Robert
Student B: Dr. Harbinger of the Stroke Team
Situation: Dr. Harbinger has arrived and asks Robert to give him a summary of Mrs. Marshall's case so far, including past medical history, present complaint, history of present complaint, medications, etc. Dr. Harbinger asks follow-up questions to clarify doubts and obtain further details about the case.

b Listen to the actual conversation between Robert and Dr. Harbinger of the Stroke Team. Check that you included all the points in your role play.

CD
T-26

c Listen to the second part of the conversation and fill in the gaps in Mrs. Marshall's notes.

CD
T-27

PHYSICAL SIGNS

Cardio-vascular:	No murmurs, rubs*, or gallops*
Neuro -	
Mental status:	Alert
Cranial nerves:	Mild facial droop* on (1) _____
Visual fields:	Profound right VF deficit*
Motor:	Drift* of right arm and leg
Sensory:	Decreased (2) _____ on right
Speech:	Moderate expressive aphasia*
Cerebellar:	NAD*

LAB RESULTS

Glucose:	(3) _____
INR:*	(4) _____
Platelets:	(5) _____

CT SCAN
No acute hemorrhagic infarct or subarachnoid* blood. No evidence of (6) _____ neoplasm,* arteriovenous malformation,* or aneurysm.*

ECG
Absence of R waves in the anterior precordial leads consistent with previous (7) _____ infarct.

d Read the following text. What further questions would you want to ask before prescribing thrombolytics for Mrs. Marshall? What additional tests would you order?

Contraindications to the use of thrombolytics

It has been shown that medications that dissolve blood clots, or thrombolytics, if administered correctly, can improve recovery from a stroke. Thrombolytics are most effective when administered within three hours of the cerebro-vascular accident. However, these medications are not without risks and the physician must ensure that the patient does not have any of the following contraindications:

1. Rapidly improving or minor symptoms

2. Evidence of intracranial hemorrhage on pre-treatment exam

3. History of intracranial hemorrhage

4. Suspicion of subarachnoid* hemorrhage

5. Recent intracranial surgery, serious head trauma or recent previous stroke (<3 months)

6. Major surgery or serious trauma excluding head trauma in the previous 14 days

7. On repeated measurements, systolic blood pressure >185 mmHg or diastolic blood pressure >110 mmHg at the time treatment is to begin. Patients require aggressive treatment to reduce blood pressure to within these limits.

8. Seizure* at onset of stroke

9. Active internal bleeding

10. History of gastrointestinal or urinary tract hemorrhage within 21 days

11. Recent lumbar puncture

12. Inracranial neoplasm,* arteriovenous malformation, or aneurysm*

13. Known bleeding diathesis,* including, but not limited to:
    - current use of oral anticoagulants* (e.g. warfarin sodium) or recent use, with international normalized ratio (INR) >1.2
    - administration of Heparin within 48 hours preceding the onset of the stroke or an elevated activated Partial Thromboplastin Time (aPTT)* at presentation
    - platelet* count <100,000 mm3

14. Abnormal blood glucose (<50 or >400mg/dL)

15. Post myocardial infarction pericarditis

(Source:http://www.guideline.gov/summary/summary.aspx?ss=15&doc_id=3422&nbr=2648)

---

 e Robert needs to explain the risks and benefits of thrombolytic agents to Mr. Marshall. Role-play the situation using the information in the following text to help you.

Thrombolytic Agents in the Treatment of Ischemic Strokes: Benefits and Risks

There are two types of stroke: ischemic and hemorrhagic. Ischemic stokes are caused when one of the major arteries to the brain is occluded* by a thrombus.*

Studies have shown that selected patients with ischemic strokes who are given thrombolytic agents within three hours of the cerebro-vascular accident are 33% more likely to have a near normal NIH stroke index after three months than patients who receive no treatment.

The principal risk from thrombolytic agents is symptomatic intracranial hemorrhage. 6.4% of patients who took thrombolytics had an intra-cerebral hemorrhage as opposed to 0.6% who were given the placebo. 75% of patients who suffer symptomatic intracranial hemorrhage die within three months.

Although thrombolytics are potentially highly beneficial to the patient, they are not without their risks. It is therefore highly advisable to have an open discussion with the patient and relatives, outlining the benefits and risks, before a decision is taken to administer thrombolytics.

(Source: The National Institute of Neurological Disorders and Stroke rt-PA Stroke Study Group. Tissue plasminogen activator for acute ischemic stroke. N Engl J Med 1995;333:1581-7.)

Lesson 5
Let's decide your rehabilitation plan

a Some 24 hours have passed and Mrs. Marshall is making a good recovery. Some decisions now have to be made about her rehabilitation plan. Write the sentences below in the correct boxes in the flow chart.

Plan home/community based treatment.
Transfer patient to nursing home.*
Plan inpatient rehabilitation program.
Plan outpatient rehabilitation program.
No treatment required. Discharge.

Does patient need rehabilitation?	➡ No ➡	1)
Yes ⬇		
Is rehabilitation likely to succeed?	➡ No ➡	2)
Yes ⬇		
Is inpatient rehabilitation indicated?	➡ Yes ➡	3)
No ⬇		
Can the patient travel to hospital daily for outpatient therapy?	➡ Yes ➡	4)
	➡ No ➡	5)

(Source: http://www.oqp.med.va.gov/cpg/STR/str_cpg/algoCframeset.htm)

b Work in groups of four. You have to decide Mrs. Marshall's rehabilitation plan. Role-play a discussion between Mr. Marshall, Mrs. Marshall, Dr. Oliveira, and Dr. Harbinger. Use the flow chart above and the following points.

Assessment of rehabilitation needs:

Communication impairment
Motor impairment
Cognitive deficit
Visual deficiency
Psychological / emotional deficit
Sensory deficit
Family caregiver support

Read the article and answer the questions.

The Role of Physical Therapy in Stroke Rehabilitation

Physical therapists specialize in treating disabilities related to motor and sensory impairments. They are trained in all aspects of anatomy and physiology related to normal function, with an emphasis on movement. They assess the stroke survivor's strength, endurance, range* of motion, gait* abnormalities, and sensory deficits to design individualized rehabilitation programs aimed at regaining control over motor functions.

Physical therapists help stroke survivors regain the use of stroke-impaired limbs, teach compensatory strategies to reduce the effect of remaining deficits, and establish ongoing exercise programs to help people retain their newly learned skills. Disabled people tend to avoid using impaired limbs, a behavior called learned non-use. However, the repetitive use of impaired limbs encourages brain plasticity* and helps reduce disabilities.

Strategies used by physical therapists to encourage the use of impaired limbs include selective sensory stimulation such as tapping or stroking, active and passive range-of-motion exercises, and temporary restraint of healthy limbs while practicing motor tasks. Some physical therapists may use a new technology, transcutaneous electrical nerve stimulation (TENS), that encourages brain reorganization and recovery of function. TENS involves using a small probe* that generates an electrical current to stimulate nerve activity in stroke-impaired limbs.

In general, physical therapy emphasizes practicing isolated movements, repeatedly changing from one kind of movement to another, and later rehearsing complex movements that require a great deal of coordination and balance, such as walking up or down stairs or moving safely between obstacles. People too weak to bear their own weight can still practice repetitive movements during hydrotherapy (in which water provides sensory stimulation as well as weight support) or while being partially supported by a harness.*

Physical therapists frequently employ selective sensory stimulation to encourage use of impaired limbs and to help survivors with neglect* regain awareness of stimuli on the neglected side of the body.

A recent trend in physical therapy emphasizes the effectiveness of engaging in goal-directed activities, such as playing games, to promote coordination.

(Adapted from http://www.ninds.nih.gov/disorders/stroke/poststrokerehab.htm#professionals)

1. Derivatives of the verb *impair* are used seven times in the article. What are the forms of the noun and the adjective? What does the adjective mean?
2. In your own words, describe three ways in which physical therapists help stroke survivors.
3. Why do you think physical therapists use "temporary restraint of healthy limbs"?
4. Two new developments in physical therapy are mentioned in the article. What are they?
5. Why do you think "goal-directed activities" might be effective?

Lesson 6
I'm going to teach you some exercises

a   Mrs. Marshall is starting physical therapy. Write the words in the box under the correct picture.

bend	grip	stretch	turn	straighten	drop	lift	push on

1. _____   2. _____   3. _____   4. _____

5. _____   6. _____   7. _____   8. _____

b   Check ✔ the correct word combinations in the table below.

	your hand	my hand	your arm	your head	your wrist
bend			✔	✔	✔
grip					
stretch					
turn					
straighten					
drop					
lift					
push on					

54   Unit 4

C Match the technical description, the illustration, and the physical therapist's instructions.

Technical description	Illustration	Instructions
1. _____ Perform posterior glide mobilizations* with the UE* at 90° of abduction.* These techniques are performed in 5 sets.* Oscillations are held up to 60 seconds with a 10 to 15 second rest in between mobilizations.	**a.**	**i** First, I want you to grip this weight and then I want you to lift up your arm in front of you so that it is horizontal. Hold it there and then drop your arm down again and rest.
2. _____ Perform passive flexion* and internal rotation UE. Each of these motions is brought to end range* and held for 20 seconds, 5 times each.	**b.**	**ii** Lift your arm out sideways so that it is level with your shoulder. Now move your arm back as far as it will go. I'll help you. Hold it there for a minute then rest for a short time. OK, now let's do it another four times.
3. _____ Perform a resisted anterior glide* to the glenohumeral joint.*	**c.**	**iii** Right, start with your arm bent. Now straighten it and then turn your hand inwards as far as it will go. Hold it there until I tell you. OK, now relax and let's do it again.

d Role-play giving instructions in non-technical language for the following procedures.

Student A: Physical therapist
Student B: Patient

Procedure:
The patient's forearm is brought into pronation,* and passive extensions* are performed at the radiocarpal* joint.

Student A: Patient
Student B: Physical therapist

Procedure:
The wrist is brought into supination* and dorsal* glides are performed at the radiocarpal* joint followed by passive wrist rotation.

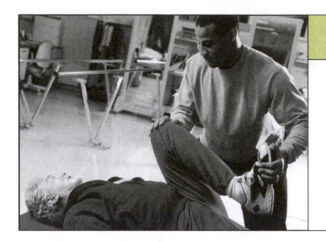

HEALTH CARE PROFESSIONALS

There are many different health care professionals involved in the rehabilitation of stroke victims.

These include rehabilitation nurses, speech therapists, physical therapists, occupational therapists, and vocational therapists.

A Research and Presentation Phases

Work in groups of three or four and choose one of the professions that are involved in the rehabilitation of stroke victims.

Research the following questions:
- What subjects do they study in their training?
- How long is the training?
- Apart from stroke victims, what other type of patients do they treat?
- What general techniques do they use?
- What techniques do they use specifically for stroke victims?
- How much do they earn in the USA and the UK?

Prepare a 5-minute presentation for the other groups.

Use pictures if necessary.

Useful Key Words
occupational therapist
speech therapist
vocational therapist
physical therapist
rehabilitation nurse

B Role-play

Form groups so that there is one member of the original groups in each new group.

Read the following case.

> Mr. Belamy is a 75-year-old retired banker. He lives with his 77-year-old wife who has rheumatoid arthritis in her hands but is otherwise healthy. They live in an upstairs apartment and rely on their car to go shopping. Their only son lives abroad with his young family.
>
> Mr. Belamy had a stroke three days ago. He had thrombolytics and is making good progress but his right arm and leg are very weak and he can't walk. Small manual tasks, like buttoning his pajamas, are causing him problems. Because of her arthritis, his wife can't help him.
>
> He is alert but has slurred* speech.

Use the flow chart in Lesson 5, exercise a, page 52 to write a rehabilitation plan for Mr. Belamy.

Unit 5

Referring a patient

I can't put up with the pain

a Read the first part of the consultation and write the questions you think Dr. Murray asks his patient.

Miss Moreno: Good morning, Dr. Murray.

Dr. Murray: Good morning, Lucia.

(1) _____

Miss Moreno: Yes, I'm still at college. I'm doing my Master's now. Almost finished, thank goodness!

Dr. Murray: (2) _____

Miss Moreno: Well, doctor, I have this earache. I tried to play it down at first but it started to get really painful. Now, I can't put up with it any more. I put it down to the cold weather but it just won't go away, so I decided to stop by and see you.

Dr. Murray: (3) _____

_____

Miss Moreno: Oh, I'm not sure exactly. Maybe about two or three months ago. I put off coming to see you because I hoped it might go away.

Dr. Murray: (4) _____

Miss Moreno: Well, it's there pretty much all the time. It's really hard to study when it's hurting all the time.

Dr. Murray: (5) _____

Miss Moreno: Well, it's sort of like a dull ache.

Dr. Murray: (6) _____

Miss Moreno: No, that's one good thing. I can sleep at night. But . . .

b Read Miss Moreno's notes and write the other questions you think Dr. Murray asked in your notebook. Then role-play the whole consultation.

LAST NAME: *Moreno*   FIRST NAME: *Lucia*   AGE: *27*

OCCUPATION: *Student*   MARITAL STATUS: *Single*

CHIEF COMPLAINT: *Earache on R.*

HISTORY OF PRESENT CONDITION:
Onset: 2/12 to 3/12 ago. Described as "dull ache." Radiates to side of face and temporal* region. No alleviating factors. Worse in evenings. No previous occurrence. Denies tinnitus*or exudates.* Reports no hearing loss. No recent trauma. No swallowing problems. Minor headaches.

PAST MEDICAL HISTORY: *Minor ailments*

MEDICATION: *Oral contraceptive*

FAMILY HISTORY: *None*

SOCIAL HISTORY: *Smokes one pack of cigarettes per day. Social drinker.*

c Underline the following phrasal verbs in the consultation in exercise **a**. Then match the phrasal verbs with their definitions in the table.

Phrasal verb	Definition
1. _____ play something down	a. to visit
2. _____ put up with something	b. to postpone
3. _____ put something down to	c. to persevere with
4. _____ go away	d. to stop, not return
5. _____ stop by	e. to minimize, to understate
6. _____ put off	f. to tolerate
7. _____ stick at something	g. to attribute, to blame something on

d Replace the phrasal verbs (in italics) in the following consultation with words from the box. The first one has been done for you.

~~contracted~~	erupt	caught	disappear	infect	lost my appetite	recovering

Doctor: So what's the problem, Mrs. Brentwall?

Patient: Well, doctor, I haven't been feeling too well recently. I *came down with* (1) _____contracted_____ a cold about a week ago and I was just *getting over it* (2) _____ when these spots started to *break out* (3) _____ on my stomach. You know, at first I thought it was something I had *picked up* (4) _____ at the gym. I rubbed some cream on the spots, but they just won't *go away* (5) _____. I'm a bit worried. Do you think I can *pass* this *on to* (6) _____ my kids?

Doctor: OK. Before I have a look, is there anything else?

Patient: Well, I've *been off* (7) _____ my food as well.

Doctor: Well, let's have a quick look and see.

e Fill in the gaps in the table.

Patient to professional (informal)	Professional to professional (formal)
1. I picked it up from my husband.	The patient contracted the illness from her husband.
2. At first, I tried to play down the problem…	
3.	The patient is recovering well from the operation.
4. I can't put up with the pain any longer.	
5.	Mr. Small blames the hot weather for his rash.
6. A classmate passed it on to me.	

a Number the boxes to put the text in order.

Otalgia*

☐ **In addition**, there is a strong association between otalgia and cancer (as high as 19%), so the physician must approach cases of otalgia with thoroughness and concern.

☐ This is **because** many nerves that supply the ear also have distributions in other parts of the head, as well as the neck and thorax.

☐ **Hence**, the list of possible causes of otalgia is lengthy.

☐ **Consequently**, a detailed history is necessary. Special attention must be paid to the examination of the patient. A complete physical examination of the head, neck, and thorax is mandatory and many cases require further special investigation, including imaging, blood testing, etc.

☐ *1* Otalgia presents a formidable diagnostic challenge for the physician.

☐ **Therefore**, disorders in these areas can refer pain to the ear and present as otalgia.

b Match the possible causes of otalgia with the appropriate examination.

Possible cause	Examination
1. Temperomandibular joint (TMJ*) dysfunction	a. Face the patient and have the patient raise the eyebrows, pucker, close the eyes, and smile.
2. Bell's palsy (Unilateral facial weakness)	b. Remove any debris* from the external auditory canal. Apply posterior and superior traction to the external auricle and insert the otoscope.
3. Ear pathology	c. Ask the patient to swallow and look for any abnormalities at the front of the neck. Then stand behind the patient and with the neck extended, palpate* the anterior aspect of the neck as the patient swallows.
4. Oral pathology	d. Under good light, perform a complete examination of the mouth. Pay special attention to the occlusion,* floor of the mouth, the under side of the tongue, and the state of the teeth and their restorations.
5. Naso-pharyngeal pathology	e. The movement of the head of the mandible* can be palpated by placing the fifth digit in the external auditory meatus* and asking the patient to open and close the mouth.
6. Thyroid pathology	f. Have the patient open the mouth, relax the tongue and breathe through the nose. Depress the tongue with a spatula* and insert the mirror.

c Role-play giving instructions for the examinations in exercise **b**. Use <u>non-technical</u> language. The first one has been done for you.
Example:

Temperomandibular joint dysfunction

OK, Now I would like to check your jaw* joint to see if there are any problems. I'm just going to put my fingers in your ears and then I would like you to open and close your mouth. OK, that's fine. Does it hurt when you open and close your mouth?

d Read the next part of Miss Moreno's notes. Decide what further investigations you would like to carry out and whether you would refer the patient.

Temp *38°C*	Respiration rate *15*	Pulse *80*	BP *110/70*

PHYSICAL EXAMINATION
Head: *No trauma*   Ears: *NAD*
Eyes: *NAD*   Nose: *NAD*
Mouth: *Poor oral hygiene. Partially erupted* lower right wisdom tooth.**
Pericoronal* inflammation. TMJ:* Slight click on right. Some tenderness* of joint.
Resp: *NAD*   CVS:* *NAD*

e Using the information from previous exercises, fill in the gaps in the following referral letter.

Dear Dr. Hoffer,

I would appreciate your advice on the management of the following patient.

Miss Lucia Moreno, a 27-year-old student, presented with (1) _____ otalgia of two to three months standing. The patient describes the pain as a (2) _____ ache, which radiates to the side of the face and the (3) _____ region. The pain progressively (4) _____ during the day. She has had no previous occurrence and (5) _____ tinnitus or exudates.

On examination, the patient was (6) _____ febrile* (100° F). Other vital signs were (7) _____. Examination of the ears, eyes, sinuses, facial muscles, nasopharyngeal tract, neck, and thorax revealed no (8) _____. However, the temperomandibular joint was tender to palpation and there was some unevenness* (9) _____ on the right. In addition, the patient has a partially (10) _____ lower right wisdom tooth with signs of pericoronal inflammation.

I would be grateful if you would see the patient and advise if you think the otalgia is of dental or TMJ origin.

Yours sincerely,

Bruce M
Bruce Murray

Lesson 3

Let's examine your mouth

 a Listen to Dr. Hoffer dictating Miss Moreno's dental chart. Fill it in, marking the restorations in the following way.

CD
T-28

 Occlusal   Disto-occlusal (DO) Mesio-occlusal (MO) Mesio-occluso-distal (MOD) Absent

RIGHT		LEFT
UPPER TEETH		

| Distal | 8 | 7 | 6 | 5 | 4 | 3 | 2 | 1 | Medial | 1 | 2 | 3 | 4 | 5 | 6 | 7 | 8 | Distal |

LOWER TEETH

 b Listen to the phone call between Dr. Hoffer and Dr. Murray and fill in the gaps in the notes.

CD
T-29

NOTES:

Patient referred with (1)_____. Poor oral hygiene. Lower right
8 impacted with(2)_____. X-ray reveals apical
radiolucency* suggesting chronic (3)_____. Lower
left 8 also (4)_____.
5 cm diameter erythematous* lesion on right(5)_____.
No cervical lymphadenopathy.*

TMJ: Slight click. Opening limited to 30mm.
Rx: Surgical removal of lower 8s. Benzodiazapines and NSAIDs* for TMJ.

---

c Using the information in the dental notes, fill in the blanks in Dr. Hoffer's letter.

Dear Doctor Murray,

In reply to your letter, dated May 19, thank you for referring the patient Lucia
Moreno.
In general, the patient has poor oral (1) _____ but her teeth are well
conserved with no evidence of caries. As you noted, she has an (2) _____
lower right 3rd molar with associated pericoronitis. (3) _____ revealed that
the lower left wisdom tooth is also impacted. I would (4) _____ removal of
both these teeth as they could be the possible cause of the otalgia.

As you noted in your letter, the (5) _____ does indeed have a small click. I noted that the patient can only (6) _____ her mouth approximately 30mm, which is also indicative of TMJ dysfunction. Radiographs revealed that there is no internal pathology of the joint. I prefer to treat TMJ dysfunction as conservatively as possible and I would therefore recommend that the patient be prescribed NSAIDs and benzodiazepines as the first line of treatment.

On (7) _____ of the soft tissues, I noted that the patient also has a small painless erythematous lesion on the right floor of the mouth. One has to be suspicious of any lesion like this and I would suggest that an excision biopsy* be performed at the same time as the third molars* are (8) _____.

In reference to our phone call today, I will be happy to arrange for treatment.

Yours sincerely,

David Hoffer

David Hoffer

💬💬 **d** Read the following notes. Role-play explaining the diagnosis, further investigations, and treatment to Miss Moreno.

Oral cancer	TMJ dysfunction	Surgical extraction of lower third molars
Oral cancer is more prevalent in the over 40s but is not unknown in a younger age group. It is a particularly dangerous cancer because diagnosis is often late when it has already spread to the cervical lymph nodes.*	It is estimated that 10% of the American population have some form of temperomandibular joint (TMJ) dysfunction. Of these, 75% are women.	Compared to the upper third molars (wisdom teeth*), the extraction of the lower third molar presents more of a challenge to the surgeon and the patient.
Diagnosis is based on clinical examination and is confirmed by biopsy.	TMJ dysfunctions can be classified into three groups: • Internal joint derangements* where there is a misalignment of the articulating surfaces of the joint. • Degenerative diseases*, which are sometimes related to trauma. • Myofascial Pain Dysfunction (MPD) which is thought to be stress related and causes pain in and around the joint involving the muscles of mastication.*	The extraction can take place under local anesthesia in the dental chair if the teeth are not badly impacted. However, it is recommended that the patient be sedated. Severely impacted eights are usually extracted under general anesthetic either on an outpatient or in-patient basis.
The success of treatment depends on the stage at which the cancer is diagnosed. Small cancers (<2cm) are highly curable by surgery or radiation with success rates between 90% and 100%. In general, for lesions <0.5 cm, excision alone is adequate if there is a margin of normal mucosa* between the lesion and the gingiva*.	Medical treatment: benzodiazepines, NSAIDs Surgical treatment: splints, orthodontics, joint replacement.	It must be made very clear to the patient that because of the local anatomy, postoperative bruising* and swelling of the face and neck are almost inevitable. It is not an operation to be undertaken lightly.

Lesson 4

Follow the postoperative advice

 a Work in pairs. Role-play the two situations below. Student **A** reads Card 1 and student **B** reads Card 2

Card 1

Student A: Dental nurse
Student B: Miss Moreno
Task: Read and memorize the preoperative instructions. Role-play giving the instructions to Miss Moreno without reading the text.

Preoperative Instructions
• Do not eat or drink anything for 8 hours prior to the appointment. If you take regular medications, take these at the normal time but with a very small sip* of water.
• You should be accompanied by a responsible adult who can take you home after the operation.
• You should not drive for 24 hours after the anesthesia.
• Wear short-sleeved clothing or clothes that can be rolled up above the elbow. Low-heeled shoes are recommended.
• Jewelry, glasses, contact lenses, and dentures must be removed before the operation.

Card 2

Student A: Miss Moreno
Student B: Dental nurse
Task: Read and memorize the following. Role-play explaining the after effects to Miss Moreno without reading the text.

After effects of Oral Surgery
The removal of impacted lower wisdom teeth is not a minor operation. You should not be alarmed by any of the following after effects:
• You will almost certainly have bruising on your cheeks and neck. This is normal. It will last about a week.
• Your face, and possibly your neck, will swell after the operation. Swelling is at its peak two to three days after the operation.
• You may feel as though you have toothache in the other teeth in front of the socket.* The pain actually comes from the socket but to you it feels as though it is coming from your other teeth. It is called referred pain.
• You could get an earache or a sore throat. Once again, this is referred pain.
• A slight fever for 24 to 48 hours after the operation is normal. If you have a high fever for longer than this, then contact the doctor.

---

b Write the postoperative instructions in the correct column.

Postoperative instructions

- Bite on a gauze pad.*
- Take the prescribed painkillers.
- Rinse your mouth vigorously.
- Drink using a straw.
- Call the doctor if you have a fever for more than 3 days postoperatively.
- Take only liquids for 24 hours postoperatively.
- Touch the wound.
- Drink alcohol for 1 week.
- Keep your mouth clean.
- Rinse your mouth for 24 hours after the operation.
- Place ice packs* against your face.
- Miss meals.

Do	Don't

 c Write the reasons for each instruction in exercise **b** in your notebook.

Example: *Don't rinse your mouth vigorously because you may wash the clot away and the socket will start to bleed.*

 d Role-play giving the postoperative instructions in exercise **b** to Miss Moreno.

Lesson 5

Your test results are back

Biopsy Report

Floor of mouth, excision biopsy; moderately differentiated squamous cell carcinoma.*

CD
T-30

a Dr. Hoffer is on the phone to a colleague. Try to fill in the gaps in their conversation. Then listen and check your answers.

Dr. Hoffer: Nelson, I wonder if I could run a case past you?

Dr. Washington: Sure, Dave. Shoot!

Dr. Hoffer: OK, It's a 27-year-old woman who (1) _____ with otalgia and was (2) _____ to me for investigation of impacted eights. I noticed a small (3) _____, about 5mm in diameter, in the floor of the mouth and so when I was doing the eights, I did an excision (4) _____ of the lesion.

Dr. Washington: And it came back positive.

Dr. Hoffer: You got it! Moderately differentiated squamous cell (5) _____.

Dr. Washington: So, let me guess, the question is whether I think (6) _____ is enough or if I would go for radiation or chemotherapy.

Dr. Hoffer: Right again.

Dr. Washington: OK. We're talking about a 5mm lesion with no cervical (7) _____ nodes.

Dr. Hoffer: And with no invasion of the gingiva.

Dr. Washington: According to my experience, radiation or chemotherapy won't make any difference in the 5-year (8) _____ rate in a 5mm lesion and the side effects* can severely affect the quality of life. If your excision biopsy had a good margin of healthy tissue, then I think your patient can be spared any more (9) _____.

Dr. Hoffer: That was exactly my plan. But it's always good to get a second (10) _____. Thanks, Nelson.

b Read the following article and answer the questions on the next page.

Oral cancer - Risk factors

75% of those diagnosed with oral cancer are smokers. When a smoker also drinks, the risks are even higher. In fact, people who both smoke and drink are up to 15 times more likely to develop oral cancer than those who don't. If you add bad oral hygiene to smoking and alcohol, then the risks become even greater.

One might think that once the patient has been diagnosed with oral cancer, it's too late to stop smoking and drinking. However, one of the characteristics of oral cancer is that there is a tendency to develop a second primary oral cancer. Approximately 15% of patients who continue to smoke and abuse alcohol after the first cancer is treated, go on to develop another oral cancer within five years. This increases to as high as 40% after five years. Moreover, patients who smoke have a lower response to radiation therapy and their survival rate is lower. It is therefore imperative that the patient change his or her lifestyle immediately

Apart from stopping smoking, moderating the use of alcohol and improving oral hygiene, a change of diet may also be beneficial. There are studies that indicate a diet low in fruits and vegetables could be a risk factor, and that conversely, one high in these foods may have a protective value against many types of cancer.

1. What four risk factors are mentioned in the article?
2. Of these, which apply to Miss Moreno?
3. Smokers have a lower response to radiation therapy. Could you use this with Miss Moreno as a reason to quit smoking? Give reasons.
4. If you were making a treatment plan for Miss Moreno, which other health care professionals would you involve?

c Role-play breaking the news to Miss Moreno. Emphasize the positive aspects of the diagnosis. Outline the treatment plan.

d Miss Moreno has to stop smoking. Read the following guidelines and then role-play a counseling session with Miss Moreno.

Supportive counseling advice	Examples
Encourage the patient in his attempt to quit.	Communicate belief in the patient's ability to quit.
	Point out that effective tobacco dependence treatments are now available.
	Point out that half of all people who have ever smoked have now quit.
Communicate caring and concern.	Ask how the patient feels about quitting.
	Directly express concern and willingness to help.
	Be open to the patient's expression of fears of quitting, difficulties experienced, and ambivalent feelings.
Encourage the patient to talk about the quitting process.	Ask about: Reasons the patient wants to quit.
	Concerns or worries about quitting.
	Success the patient has achieved.
	Difficulties encountered while trying to quit.
Provide basic information about smoking and successful quitting.	Explain: Nicotine substitutes are available.
	Any smoking (even a single puff*) increases the likelihood of full relapse.
	Withdrawal symptoms* typically peak within 1-3 weeks after quitting.
	Withdrawal symptoms include negative mood, urges to smoke, and difficulty concentrating.

(Source: Quick Reference Guide for Clinicians- Treating Tobacco Use and Dependence U.S. Department of Health & Human Services)

Lesson 6

You are very lucky

a | Read the article and answer the questions.

Brushing your teeth regularly is not just about looking good and having fresh breath, it's about staying healthy!

The effects of poor oral hygiene are widespread and serious. Apart from causing intra-oral diseases such as gingivitis,* periodontitis,* oral cancer, halitosis,* and dental caries, poor oral hygiene has been linked to heart disease, lung disease, and premature birth.

The source of all these problems is plaque, a sticky white substance that forms on teeth. If it is not removed completely from all parts of the mouth, it will infect the gingiva leading to gingivitis. Gingivitis is characterized by tender, erythematous gingival papillae,* which bleed easily. In its early stages, gingivitis is reversible and with diligent oral hygiene, the gingiva will return to good health.

However, if the papillae become swollen, they form pockets* around the teeth and it is impossible to clean inside these pockets with a toothbrush. A dentist or dental hygienist can clean inside these pockets with a special rubber brush.

If gingivitis is left untreated the plaque will infect the periodontal ligament* and cause periodontitis. Periodontitis is a slow progressive disease which causes gingival recession,* loosening of the teeth, and eventually loss of the teeth. It is possible to treat advanced periodontitis but it requires surgery and the esthetic results are not good.

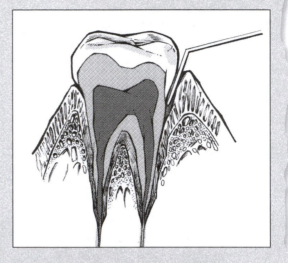

How the dental hygienist can help

First, your dentist or dental hygienist can help you identify the places in the mouth where you are not brushing properly. Then they can advise you on correct tooth brushing and flossing* techniques. In addition, he or she can remove the calculus (calcified plaque) that forms on the teeth. This is far too hard to remove with a toothbrush and needs to be scraped off with special dental instruments.

Questions
1. What title would you give this article?
2. What are the steps that lead from the formation of plaque to advanced periodontitis?
3. Write a list of what makes good oral hygiene so important.
4. Even if a patient brushes his / her teeth regularly and thoroughly, why is it necessary to go to the dentist or dental hygienist regularly?

 b | Role-play explaining the importance of oral hygiene to Miss Moreno.

c Use the pictures and the words indicated to explain to a patient how to brush his / her teeth properly.

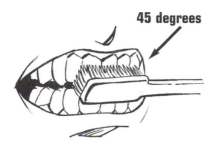

45 degrees

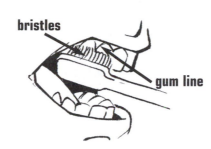

bristles

gum line

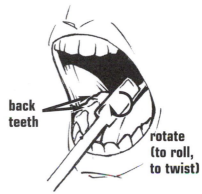

back teeth

rotate (to roll, to twist)

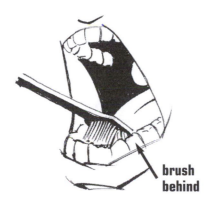

brush behind

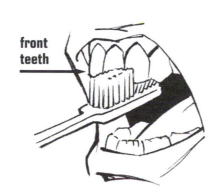

front teeth

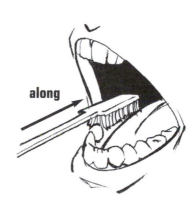

along

d Write the questions in the following dialogue.

Dr. Hoffer: So, Miss Moreno. Good to see you again. You're here for your three-month check-up, I see.
Miss Moreno: That's right.
Dr. Hoffer: (1) _____
Miss Moreno: Fine. In fact, I've never felt better in my life!
Dr. Hoffer: (2) _____
Miss Moreno: Yes, the earache went away almost immediately after you took out the teeth.
Dr. Hoffer: (3) _____
Miss Moreno: No. I've no pain at all now.
Dr. Hoffer: (4) _____
Miss Moreno: Yes. I've given up completely. It wasn't easy but I didn't give in. I should have quit years ago.
Dr. Hoffer: (5) _____
Miss Moreno: I hope so. I've been keeping up the flossing and my gums have stopped bleeding.
Dr. Hoffer: Well, congratulations, Miss Moreno. You're a very lucky lady!
Miss Moreno: Thanks to you, doctor. Thanks to you.

PREVENTATIVE HEALTH

In this unit, we saw the connection between smoking and oral cancer. Stopping smoking will reduce the chances of getting many diseases including cancer, strokes, heart disease, etc. However, there are many other measures that people can take to prevent illness, such as changing their diet or exercising appropriately.

A Research Phase

Work in groups and research the prevention of ONE of the following:

- Heart disease
- Dental caries
- Accidents at work
- Accidents in the home
- Cancer
- Road traffic accidents

Useful Key Words
preventive health
preventive medicine
prevention

OR you can choose another topic related to prevention that is relevant to your field.

B Presentation Phase

- Present your findings to the class.
- Use pictures or posters/charts to make your presentations more interesting.
- Make your presentation more interactive by asking the other students to fill in a questionnaire on their eating, smoking, drinking, and exercise habits.

Additional Resources

Unit 1   **Review**   72

Unit 2   **Review**   73

Unit 3   **Review**   74

Unit 4   **Review**   75

Unit 5   **Review**   76

Grammar Resource   77

    Question forms: Review

    Reported speech

    Verb tense review

    Modals for advice and obligation

    Modals for deduction

    Past perfect tense

    Question tags

    Passive voice (simple present and simple past)

    Phrasal verbs

Picture Dictionary   85

Glossary   92

Audio Script   97

Review 1

A Are the following questions good or bad ways of starting "small talk"?
Check ✔ the appropriate box. Compare your answers with those of a partner.

	Good	Bad	
1.	☐	☐	Good morning, Mrs. Calvini. Are you still working in the supermarket?
2.	☐	☐	So, what have you come for, Mr. Abbott?
3.	☐	☐	You're looking very tanned, Sean. Have you been on vacation?
4.	☐	☐	Good morning, Mr. Schultz. I haven't seen you down at the gym recently.
5.	☐	☐	You're looking a bit pale. What's up?

B Match the questions with the steps of a patient interview.

a. _____ Do you smoke?

b. _____ Have you ever had anything like this before?

c. _____ And has there been anything else apart from the dizziness?

d. _____ When did the problem begin?

e. _____ Does anyone else in you family have the same problem?

f. _____ So, what can we do for you?

g. _____ Are you having any other problems?

h. _____ Are you taking any pills or medicines at the moment?

i. _____ How're things at the store?

Steps

1. Introductory "small talk"
2. Chief Complaint
3. History of present
   condition
   a) onset and timing
   b) other symptoms
   c) previous occurrence
4. Past Medical History
5. Family History
6. Medication
7. Social History

C Read the case notes and write the questions that the doctor asked.

LAST NAME: **McGrayne**   LAST NAME: **John**

OCCUPATION: **1. Accountant**   AGE: **53**

MEDICATION: **2. None**

CHIEF COMPLAINT: **3. Rash on back and chest**

HISTORY OF PRESENT CONDITION:
  4. Started on chest 5. Began 2 weeks ago 6. Painless

1. *What do you do for a living?* _____
2. _____
3. _____
4. _____
5. _____
6. _____

Review 2

A Role-play the following telephone conversations.

> **Student A:** ER intern. You are waiting for a CSF glucose result. It is urgent.
> **Student B:** Lab technician. Make excuse. Apologize. Another 10 minutes.

> **Student A:** ER intern. 2- year-old has arm stuck in metal pipe. All attempts to remove it have failed. Possible to drill pipe off?
> **Student B:** Dental intern. Yes. Where? When?

B Write the verbs in the correct tense.

1. The ambulance _____ (already leave) when the second victim (discover) _____ .
2. The judge ruled that the doctor _____ (be) guilty because he _____ (not write up) the notes correctly.
3. It was not clear whether the patient _____ (take) his medication before _____ (collapse).
4. The post mortem _____ (indicate) that the patient _____ (die) from a massive heart attack.
5. The nurse _____ (already give) the patient the medication by the time the doctor _____ (arrive).

C Circle the word or expression that you think is most appropriate to use with patients.

1.	2.	3.
a) Did you vomit?	a) abdomen	a) chronic inflammation
b) Did you throw up?	b) stomach	b) long-standing inflammation
c) Were you sick?	c) belly	c) old inflammation
4.	5.	6.
a) hemorrhage	a) tracheostomy	a) aspirate some fluid
b) bleeding	b) open the trachea	b) suck out some fluid
c) loss of blood	c) cut the neck	c) extract some fluid

D Rewrite the following sentences so they are less threatening.

1. We're going to make an incision in your abdomen and aspirate the exudates.

_____

2. Your mother was knocked unconscious and suffered a fracture to the cranium.

_____

3. You're going to need major surgery, the result of which is uncertain.

_____

Review 3

A What questions would you ask to find out about the features of pain.

Features of Pain	Question
1. Location	_____
2. Duration	_____
3. Intensity & character	_____
4. Onset	_____
5. Timing	_____
6. Alleviating factors	_____
7. Aggravating factors	_____
8. Previous occurrence	_____
9. Triggering factors	_____

B Work with a partner and role-play taking a medical history.

Student A: Doctor
Student B: Patient
You have an ache in your stomach which started yesterday evening and has been getting worse. At first, you had cramps but now the pain is continuous. It is around your navel. You tried indigestion pills but they made you vomit and you have also been getting diarrhea.

Student B: Doctor
Student A: Patient
You have an excruciating pain that starts at the side of your lower back and goes round your side. Sometimes it goes down your leg. It started two days ago and it comes and goes. You have never had pain like this before and you never want pain like it again!

C Write the verbs in parentheses in either the active or passive voice.

Isaac's syndrome, also (1) _____ (know) as neuromyotonia, is a rare neuromuscular disorder (2) _____ (cause) by the nerve fibers constantly sending signals to the muscles. The muscles (3) _____ (stimulate) constantly and the patient (4) _____ (suffer) from repeated spasms. Other symptoms (5) _____ (include) increased sweating and occasionally, sensory loss. Speech and breathing (6) _____ (affect) if the pharyngeal muscles (7) _____ (involve).

Relief from the spasms and pain (8) _____ (provide) by anticonvulsants but there (9) _____ (be) no cure.

Review 4

A Rewrite the following colloquial sentences in formal English.

1. He's doing real good.

_____

2. I guess it started paining me about two weeks back.

_____

3. You bet I can't touch my toes. I can't hardly touch my knees!

_____

B Write five questions you would ask the following patients' relatives.

| **Case 1:** |
| An unconscious patient who appears to have had an epileptic seizure. |

| **Case 2:** |
| A six-month-old baby with acute diarrhea. |

C Work with a partner and role-play Case 1 in Exercise B. Reverse roles for Case 2.

D Write the full form of the following abbreviations.

Abbreviations	Full form
1. MI	
2. CC	
3. HPC	
4. PMH	
5. VF	
6. 2/12	

E Write the following words in a sentence.

1. rehabilitation _____
2. therapy _____
3. ischemic _____
4. proximal _____
5. tourniquet _____

F Write how you would explain this procedure to a patient.

Perform passive flexion and external rotation UE. Each of these motions is brought to end range and held for 10 seconds, 5 times each.

_____

_____

_____

Review 5

A Rewrite the following sentences without the phrasal verbs.

1. Miss Moreno has gotten over her illnesses now.

_____

2. She regrets putting off going to see the dentist.

_____

3. The pain after her operation was terrible but she put up with it.

_____

4. It wasn't easy quitting smoking but she stuck with it.

_____

B Fill in the blanks using the words in the box.

because	in addition	therefore

1. The lingual nerve supplies both the ear and the floor of the mouth. _____, pain from a lesion on the floor of the mouth can be referred to the ear.
2. _____ to smoking, poor oral hygiene is an important cause of oral cancer.
3. _____ of the threat of cancer, a biopsy was performed immediately.

C Write a referral letter to a physician using the information from the patient's dental notes. Give it to a classmate.

DENTAL NOTES			
Last Name:	First name:	Age:	Occupation:
Devon	Ellis	56	Bus driver

11/ 11	CC: halitosis 3/12. Noted by spouse. SHx: 20 cigarettes per day for > 20 years O/E: Oral hygiene excellent. Full dentition, no dental restorations. No gingivitis, periodontal disease or caries. Nicotine staining of teeth. Soft tissues healthy. Strong halitosis but appears not caused by oral pathology. ?? pathology of respiratory tract, ?? liver disease.

D Read your classmate's letter and write a reply. Use the information below.

- **Halitosis.**
- Halitosis can be divided into three types: intra-oral, extra-oral and psychogenic.
- **Investigations for extra-oral halitosis**
- Endoscopy for the sinus and nasopharyngeal pathology.
- CT scan to exclude nasal obstruction, respiratory tract disorders (neoplasm, infection, etc.)
- Blood and urine investigations to rule out diabetes, infection, allergies, metabolic disorders.

Grammar Resource

Question forms (review)   78

Reported speech   79

Past simple vs. past continuous tense   80

Past perfect tense   81

Modals for deduction   82

Tag questions   83

Passive voice   84

Phrasal verbs   85

Review: Question forms

Yes/no question	Short answer	
Do you feel any pain?	Yes, I do.	No, I don't.
Does anyone in your family have the same problem?	Yes, my son does.	No, they don't.
Can you turn your head to the left?	Yes, I can.	No, I can't
Wh- question	**Answer**	
Why are you here today?	I'm having trouble walking.	
What seems to be the trouble?	I think I've hurt my foot.	
When did you first notice the ringing in your ears?	Two days ago.	
Where does it hurt?	In the middle of my back.	
How would you describe the pain?	It comes and goes.	

- *Wh-* questions start with *who, what, where, when, why* or *how.*
- *Wh-* questions always require a longer answer.

PRACTICE

Read the patient's answers below. Write the doctor's questions.

1. Q: _____

   A: Yes, I do. I smoke a pack of cigarettes a day.

2. Q: _____

   A: I have this lump on the back of my neck.

3. Q: _____

   A: It hurts when you touch it right there.

4. Q: _____

   A: Yes, I do. I'm allergic to penicillin.

5. Q: _____

   A: Yes, I do. I run five miles a day.

ABOUT YOU Think about your most recent doctor's appointment. Write down at least three questions the doctor asked you.

_____

_____

_____

Reported speech

Direct speech	Reported speech
"You **don't get** enough exercise."	The doctor **said** (that) **I didn't get** enough exercise.
"Your test results **are** inconclusive."	The doctor **told me** (that) **my** test results **were** inconclusive.
"Please sit down."	The nurse **asked me** to sit down.

- Reported speech reports what someone has said.
- The use of *that* is optional.
- Some reporting verbs e.g. *tell* must be followed by an indirect object or pronoun.
- Change the present tense in direct speech to the past tense in reported speech.
- Change the pronouns to reflect the correct person.

Some verbs commonly used in reported speech				Verbs commonly used in reported speech that take an indirect object or pronoun			
say	agree	complain	explain	tell	ask	assure	advise
reply	state	answer		convince	promise	remind	teach

PRACTICE

Imagine you are reporting what a doctor told you during a consultation. Change the direct speech to reported speech.

1. "Do you have any family history of diabetes?"

    The doctor asked me if I had any family history of diabetes.

2. "Your temperature is a little high."

    _____

3. "Can you roll up your sleeve."

    _____

4. "Please stand over here."

    _____

5. "You can exercise normally during the treatment."

    _____

ABOUT YOU Think about a recent conversation you have had. Retell it in reported speech.

_____

_____

_____

_____

Past continuous vs. simple past

Past continuous	Subject + *was / were* + present participle
Affirmative statement	**I was** just **finishing** the night shift when an emergency case came in. Subject + *was / were* + present participle
Negative statement	**He wasn't complaining** about the pain until we got here. Subject + *was / were* + *not* + present participle
Yes/no questions	**Were you leaving** the hospital when the patient arrived? *Was / were* + subject + present participle
Wh- questions	**What was she doing** when she fainted? *Wh-* word + *was / were* + subject + present participle

- Use the past continuous to talk about actions that were already in progress at a given time in the past.
- The past continuous is not used on its own very often. It is frequently used together with the simple past to show that one action began and was in progress when another action happened.
  In these situations, the adverbs *when* and *while* are often used.
  > **While** *I was finishing a ward round, a new patient came into Emergency.*
  > *Doctor Plantz was just leaving the hospital* **when** *the ambulance arrived.*

PRACTICE 1

Complete this text about a medical intern's first night shift using the verb in parentheses in the correct form

When I _____ (arrive) at the Emergency Department for my first night shift, several patients and their relatives_____ (wait) to be attended. A nurse_____ (look for) the relatives of a patient who had just been admitted. A doctor _____ (ask for) some test results. A child _____ (cry) while a nurse_____ (try) to take a blood sample. Some nurses _____ (leave) the hospital after finishing work and the night staff _____ (start) their shifts.

PRACTICE 2

Write sentences about two events using the simple past and the past continuous. Use *when* or *while*.

1. me / just finish / they / call / ward round / to emergency / I
   _____ *I was just finishing a ward round when they called me to emergency* _____
2. my e -mails / arrive / wait for / patient / check / I

   _____

3. She / work / the garden / start / feel ill / she

   _____

4. he / cough / wheeze / patient / the consulting room / come into

   _____

5. have surgery / he / his relatives / outside / wait

   _____

Past perfect tense

Past perfect	Subject + *had* + past participle
Affirmative statement	**The doctor had explained** the tests when the nurse arrived. Subject + *had* + past participle
Negative statement	**I had not expected** to leave the hospital so soon after surgery. Subject + *had* + *not* + past participle
Yes/no questions	**Had you explained** the procedure before? *Had* + subject + past participle
Wh- questions	**What had you eaten** before you started feeling ill? *Wh-* word + *had* + subject + past participle

- Use the past perfect to talk about an action that was completed before another action or time in the past or to explain why this event happened.

- The past perfect is used for the earlier action, and the simple past for the later action.

- With *before* and *after*, the present perfect isn't necessary because the time relationship has already been established.
  Before *Julia finished work, she started to feel ill.*
  After *the operation, they took me back to my room.*

PRACTICE 1

Read the sentences and circle the correct verb forms.

1. I (just finished / had just finished) work when I (started / had started) to feel dizzy.

2. Susana (was / had been) worried about the operation. She (never had / had never had) surgery before.

3. By the time he (arrived / had arrived) at the hospital, his wife (had / had had) the baby.

4. The patient (complained / had complained) that he (didn't eat / hadn't eaten) before coming to the hospital.

PRACTICE 2

Complete the text below with the verbs in the correct tense (simple past or past perfect).

I _____ (check into) the hospital in the afternoon. I _____ (be) worried because I _____ (never have) surgery before and I _____ (not know) what to expect. But Jake _____ (stay) with me until they_____ (tell) him that he had to leave. By evening, I _____ (already prepare) for the operation. I _____ (wait) for them to take me the operating theater. Before I _____ (know) it, the operation was over and I _____ (be) back in my room. Someone _____ (leave) some flowers and a card in my room. They_____ (be) from Jake.

Modals for deduction

Example	Explanation
The patient has a mild fever and a cough. It **could** / **might** / **may** be a viral infection.	*Could, might and may* can be used to say that a situation is possible. In this example, there are other possible diagnoses (besides the viral infection).
With these levels of glucose, it **must** be diabetes.	*Must* can be used when we have a high level of certainty about a particular situation. In this case, the level of glucose indicates that other possibilities have been eliminated. We can be fairly certain that the patient has diabetes.
The tests came back negative. It **can't** be meningitis.	The opposite of *must* for expressing a high degree of certainty about something is *can't*. In this case, the tests done to check the diagnosis of meningitis were negative. We can be fairly sure the patient doesn't have the disease.

- We can also use **it is likely / unlikely** to express strong possibility.

  There is no known family history. **It's unlikely** *to be hereditary.*
  It's likely *that she picked it up at school. A lot of her classmates are ill.*

PRACTICE 1

Write *Do you think* questions with the following modals.

1. might / have an infection

   Do you think my son might have an infection?

2. could / take a pain killer

3. may / have hurt the tendon

4. might / need tests

PRACTICE 2

Use modal verbs to make deductions about the following situations.

1. She's wheezing and in obvious respiratory distress.

   She might have bronchiolitis.

2. The patient has diarrhea, nausea and stomach pain.

3. Susan has been sneezing all morning.

4. There are differences in percussion between each side of the chest.

Tag questions: Present, past and future tenses

Tense	Affirmative statement	Negative tag ending	Answer	
Simple present	You work,	don't you?	Yes, I do.	No, I don't.
Present continuous	You are working,	aren't you?	Yes, I am.	No, I'm not.
Simple past	They talked,	didn't they?	Yes, they did.	No, they didn't.
Past continuous	They were talking,	weren't they?	Yes, they were.	No, they weren't.
Present perfect	They have talked,	haven't they?	Yes, they have.	No, they haven't.
Past perfect	They had talked,	hadn't they?	Yes, they had.	No, they hadn't.
Future	You will talk,	won't you?	Yes, we will.	No, we won't.

- Tag questions are used to check if something is true.
- A tag question uses an auxiliary verb + a pronoun.
- A tag question uses the same tense as the main verb.
- A tag question can consist of a negative statement, and an affirmative tag question:

    *You don't **work**, **do** you?*

PRACTICE

Match the tag questions to the statements

1. He was informed of the procedure, _____
2. Roberto didn't do a good job, _____
3. The hospital was offering free screening, _____
4. I haven't been late for any appointments, _____
5. Sarah had worked hard, _____
6. They arrived a few minutes late for work, _____
7. You haven't been exercising lately, _____
8. I was at that meeting, _____
9. We had increased the hospital's efficiency, _____
10. She has taken on more responsibility, _____

a. hadn't she?
b. wasn't he?
c. wasn't it?
d. didn't they?
e. didn't we?
f. have you?
g. hasn't she?
h. hadn't we?
i. wasn't I?
j. have I?
k. did he?

ABOUT YOU   Add a tag question to each statement. Then answer the questions so they are true for you.

1. You are always on time for class, _____   A: _____
2. You do exercise, _____   A: _____
3. You try to maintain a healthy diet, _____   A: _____
4. Your grades were great last semester, _____   A: _____

The passive voice

Passive voice	Subject + *be* + past participle (+ *by* agent)
Affirmative statement	**Operations are performed** everyday (by surgeons). Subject + *be* + past participle
Negative statement	**I was not told** about the meeting (by the chief resident). Subject + *be* + *not* + past participle
Yes/no questions	**Were radiographs taken?** *Be* + subject + past participle
Wh- questions	**When was the donor organ delivered**? *Wh-* word + *be* + subject + past participle

- The passive voice can be used with any verb tense. The form of the verb *to be* is changed to indicate the tense.

   *The hospital **was** built in 1965.* (past simple)
   *The fracture **is being** set at the moment.* (present continuous)
   *She **has been** moved to another ward.* (present perfect)
   *The doctor **will be** finished shortly.* (*will* future)

- Sentences in the passive voice talk mainly about the result of the action, not the person who does the action (the agent).

- Include the agent in the sentence only if this information is important.

   *The surgery was performed **by Dr. Church.***

PRACTICE 1
Rewrite each sentence in the passive voice.

1. Dr. Rowlings referred the patient for further tests.

   _____

2. We removed the stitches on his last visit.

   _____

3. Dr. Marshall examined the patient.

   _____

4. We ran some routine tests.

   _____

5. Stroke patients usually require extensive postoperative care.

   _____

PRACTICE 2
Fill in the correct form of the verb in the active or passive voice.

1. We _____(do) a biopsy after finding a lesion inside her mouth.
2. The doctor_____(test) the patient's reflexes.
3. This condition _____(treat) with antibiotics.
4. Depression_____(present) in many of these cases.
5. Dr. Murray _____(examine) the patient.
6. The patient_____(complain) of a intense stabbing pain in his back.

Phrasal verbs

Example	Explanation
He **wrote down** the dose. I can't **put up with** the pain any longer.	Two-part phrasal verbs consist of a verb + preposition and / or adverb.
Let's **call in** a specialist. Let's **call** a specialist **in**. Let's **call** her **in**.	Some two-part phrasal verbs can be separated by a noun or pronoun. If a pronoun is used, it must separate the parts of the verb.
Don't **give up** now. You have almost finished your treatment.	Some two-part phrasal verbs cannot be separated.
We need to **come up with** an explanation for the problem.	Multi-word verbs consist of a verb, an adverb and a preposition. They can never be separated and always take a direct object.

- Some two-part phrasal verbs can be separated: **call in / up, fill out, leave out, put on, set up, turn on, write down.**
- Some two-part phrasal verbs cannot be separated: **look into, show up, keep on, give up / in.**

PRACTICE 1

Underline the correct sentence. If both are correct, underline both of them.

1. I wrote down the correct dose. / I wrote the correct dose down.

2. He left out the test results. / He left the test results out.

3. Did they ever look into the cause of the fever? / Did they ever look the cause of the fever into?

4. If you can't put the pain up with, we'll call in a specialist. / If you can't put up with the pain, we'll call in a specialist.

PRACTICE 2

Rewrite each sentence using a pronoun instead of the underlined noun.

1. You can turn on <u>the machine</u>. _____

2. She set up <u>two appointments</u>. _____

3. You should put on <u>the robe</u>. _____

4. We need to call in <u>a specialist</u>. _____

5. Please fill out the <u>insurance form</u>. _____

Picture Dictionary

1 Surface Anatomy   87

2 The Human Skeleton   88

3 General Anatomy   89

4 Medical Instruments   90

5 Nursing Procedures   91

Surface Anatomy

CD
T-31

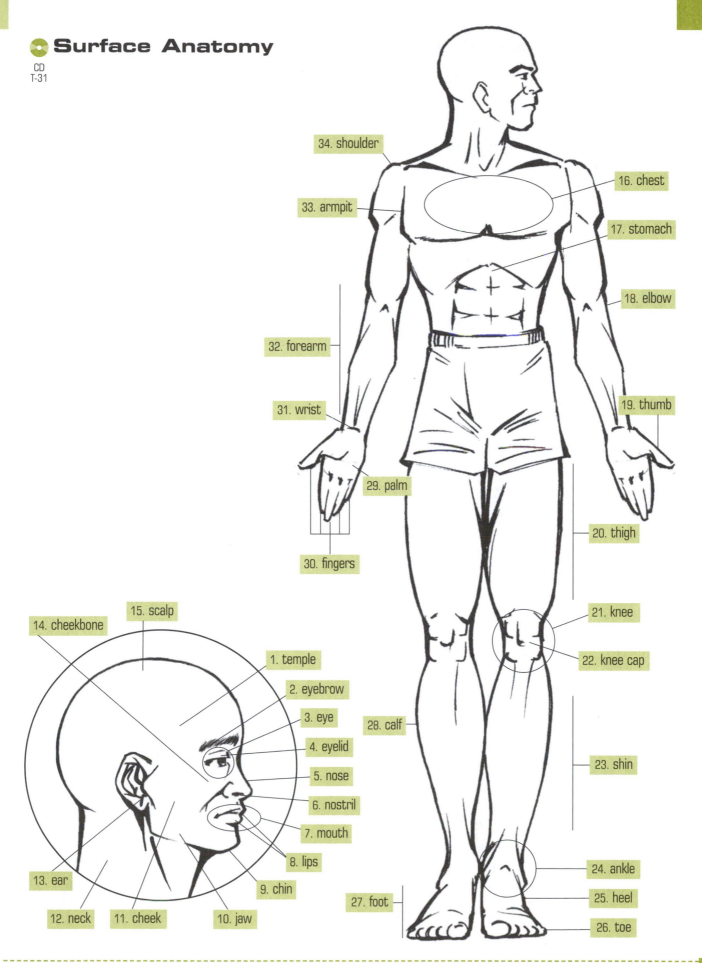

34. shoulder
16. chest
33. armpit
17. stomach
18. elbow
32. forearm
31. wrist
19. thumb
29. palm
20. thigh
30. fingers
21. knee
22. knee cap
28. calf
23. shin
15. scalp
14. cheekbone
1. temple
2. eyebrow
3. eye
4. eyelid
5. nose
6. nostril
7. mouth
8. lips
13. ear
9. chin
12. neck
11. cheek
10. jaw
24. ankle
27. foot
25. heel
26. toe

● The Human Skeleton

CD
T-32

Medical term	Lay term
1. cranium	skull
2. mandible	jaw bone
3. clavicle	collar bone
4. sternum	breast bone
5. humerus	arm
6. a) radius, b) ulna	forearm
7. pelvic girdle	hip bone
8. femur	thigh bone
9. patella	knee cap
10. a) tibia, b) fibula	shinbone
11. cervical spine	neck bone
12. scapula	shoulder blade
13. rib cage	ribs
14. spine	back bone

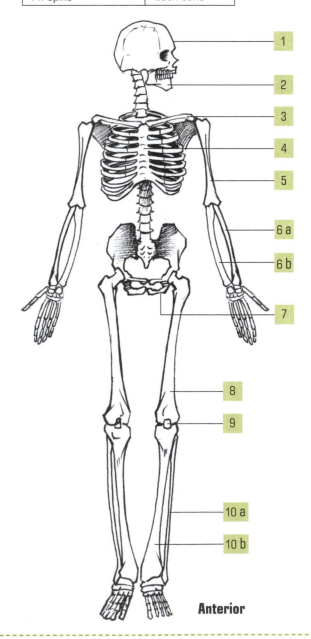

Anterior

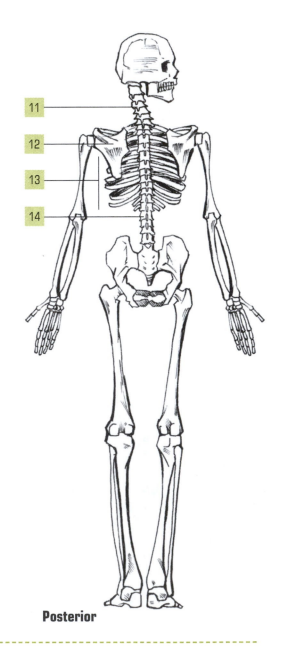

Posterior

● General Anatomy

CD
T-33

1. brain
2. brain stem
3. neuron
4. heart
5. aortic arch
6. trachea
7. lungs
8. esophagus
9. stomach
10. small intestine
11. colon
12. liver
13. pancreas
14. kidneys
15. ureter
16. bladder
17. ovaries
18. fallopian tubes
19. uterus

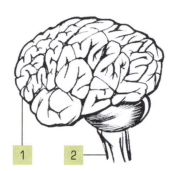

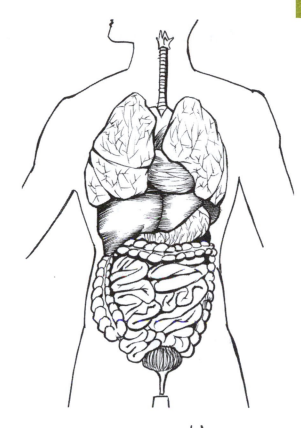

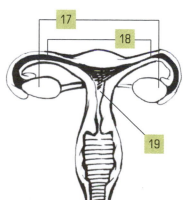

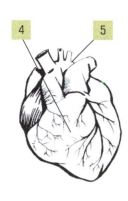

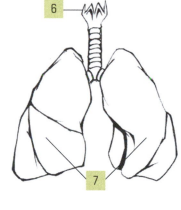

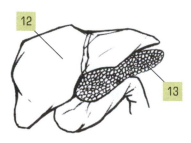

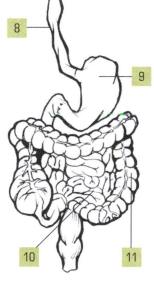

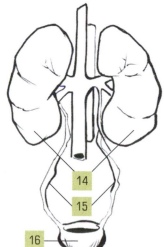

Medical Instruments

CD
T-34

Instruments
1. stethoscope
2. thermometer
3. sphygmomanometer
4. otoscope
5. ophthalmoscope
6. reflex hammer
7. dental probe
8. dental mirror
9. clamps
10. scalpel

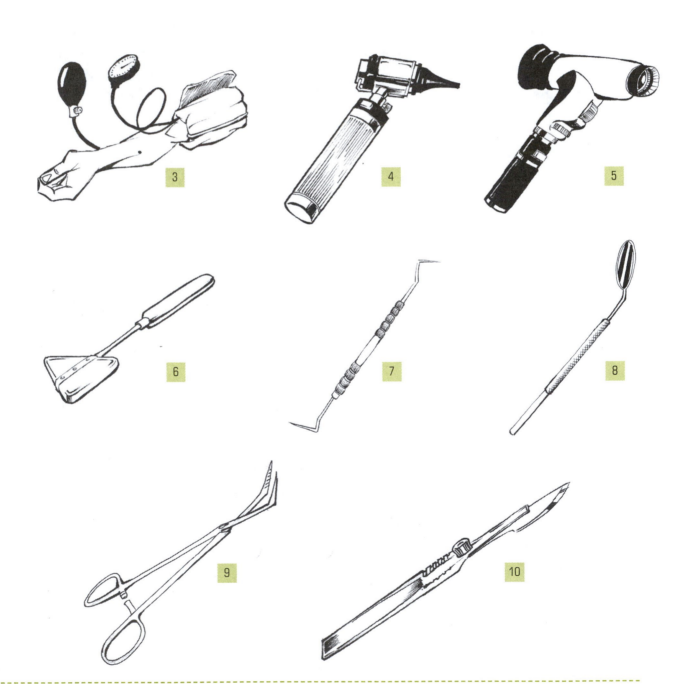

Nursing Procedures

CD
T-35

Procedures
1. applying a bandage or dressing a wound
2. administering an injection or vaccine
3. administering oxygen
4. performing adult cardiopulmonary resuscitation
5. setting up an intravenous drip

1

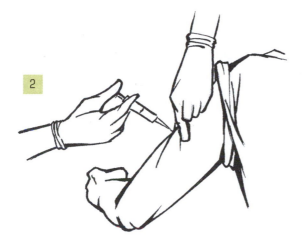

2

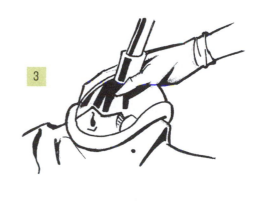

3

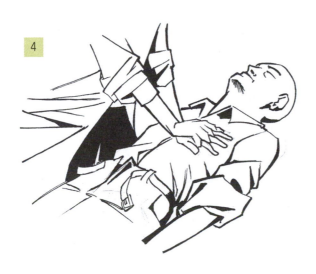

4

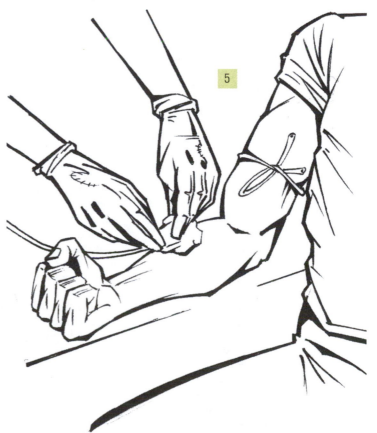

5

Glossary

Unit 1

bias *n*	a statistical sampling or testing error caused by systematically favoring some outcomes over others
bind *v*	to stick together
breathlessness *n*	a lack or shortage of breath
celiac disease *n*	disease caused by an allergic reaction in the intestine to a protein (gluten) found in wheat
cephalosporin *n*	a type of antibiotic used for penicillin-resistant bacteria
clubbing *n*	thickening, usually at ends of fingers
dizziness *n*	vertigo, a feeling of being unstable, about to fall
dullness *n*	a dead sound heard when the chest is tapped
dura *n*	one of the membranes around the brain and spinal cord
dysarthria *n*	slurred, unclear speech
exophthalmus *n*	staring eyes
flaring *n*	dilating, expansion or opening of the nostrils
fasting *n*	the act or practice of abstaining from or eating very little
glucosuria *n*	presence in the urine of abnormal amounts of sugar
hemoglobin A1C test *n*	a test that shows average blood sugar throughout a two- to three-month period
hissing (in ears) *n*	tinnitus, a sound like air escaping from a tire
hot flush *n*	a hot sensation
hyperhidrosis *n*	heavy sweating
hypoglycemia *n*	low blood sugar
ketone *n*	a product of fat metabolism found in the urine of diabetic patients
lobe *n*	rounded projection of a body organ or part
lump *n*	tumor, swelling
mean *n*	average
muscle wasting *adj*	loss of the tissue of the muscles
night sweats *n*	profuse sweating during sleep
nystagmus *n*	involuntary eye movements
ophthalmoscope *n*	an instrument used to examine the eyes
oral agents *n*	medication taken by mouth
otoscope *n*	an instrument used to examine the ears
phlegm *n*	a moist excretion that protects mucus membranes, mucus
podiatrist *n*	a specialist in caring for the feet
polyphagia *n*	excessive hunger
polyuria *n*	frequent urination
rash *n*	red spots or marks on the skin
refined (sugar) *adj*	processed (white sugar)
ringing *n*	a sound like a bell in the ears
Romberg test *n*	neurological test where the patient is asked to stand with the eyes closed and the feet close together; tests poor balance
seizure *n*	an attack where the patient's body becomes rigid and collapses
sphygmamometer *n*	an instrument used for measuring blood pressure
stabbing *adj*	describing a pain like a knife entering the body
stridor *n*	a sound made when breathing out
tachycardia *n*	rapidly beating heart
tingling *n, adj*	a feeling of pins and needles, partially numb, parasthesia
tremor *n*	shaking
vertigo *n*	dizziness
vital signs *n*	temperature, blood pressure, pulse and respiration rate
weighted *adj*	adjusted to reflect value or proportion
wheezing *n*	breathing with difficulty, making a hoarse whistling sound

Unit 2

aeration *n*	supply of air to the lungs
airway *n*	the breathing passage, larynx, trachea and bronchi
bronchiolitis *n*	inflammation of the air sacks of the lungs caused by respiratory syncytial virus
inflammatory burst *n*	a rapid increase in inflammation of a tissue
c/o *n*	abbreviation for "complains of"
cachexic *adj*	underweight, thin
cascade *n*	one event leading to another and so on
cerebrospinal fluid *n*	the fluid that surrounds the brain and spinal cord
comatose *adj*	in a coma, unconscious
conjunctival *adj*	related to the conjunctiva, or membrane covering the eye
constricting *n*	tightening
cramping *n*	a painful sensation felt in the muscles after excessive exercise
crest *n*	the top or peak of a curve
cricothyrotomy *n*	a surgical operation to open the wind pipe at the front of the neck to allow the patient to breath
crown *n*	the visible part of a tooth
CSF *n*	cerebro spinal fluid
CSF / serum glucose ratio *n*	
	the ratio between the glucose level in the cerebro-spinal fluid and the glucose level in the serum.
dose *n*	the recommended amount of a drug taken by a patient
drowsy *adj*	sleepy
edema *n*	swelling caused by excessive lymph fluid in the tissues
flared *adj*	dilated, open
flex *n*	to bend
flushing *n*	a reddening of the skin
Gram's stain *n*	a stain on a microscope slide used to identify bacteria
hematoma *n*	a blood filled swelling, a bruise
hypoxemia *n*	abnormally low oxygen in the blood
intercostal *adj*	between the ribs
intubation *n*	putting a tube into a hollow organ, e.g. the trachea or esophagus
lethargy *n*	lacking energy
lever *vb*	to lift out a tooth
lignocaine *n*	a local analgesic
mandibular *adj*	referring to the mandible (jaw bone)
manometer *n*	a meter for measuring pressure
mediator *n*	a chemical released from cells as a result of the interaction between an antibody and an antigen
midline *n*	an imaginary line drawn down the center of the body
murmur *n*	a heart sound like someone speaking very quietly
non-tender *adj*	not painful
numb *v*	to make part of the body lose its ability to feel
Observation Ward *n*	a room in a hospital where patients are watched carefully
orderly *n*	a hospital worker who cleans and does chores
percussion *n*	hitting or tapping something
pericarditis *n*	inflammation around the heart
post mortem *n*	an examination performed after death
retractions *n*	drawing in of the neck and chest with each breath
retrieve *v*	to recover, to find
shift *n*	the part of the day in which a person works
short-staffed *adj*	not enough workers for the tasks to be performed
splint *v*	support or restrict with a rigid appliance (splint)
steroid *n*	a group of fat soluble compounds, e.g., progesterone, cholesterol
stitch *n*	the thread closing a wound or cut
strain *n*	a type or species of a bacterium or virus
stridor *n*	a rough vibrating sound when breathing in
subcostal *adj*	below the ribs
subdural *adj*	under one of the linings (dura mater) of the brain and spinal cord

suprasternal *adj*	above the chest bone
swelling *n*	an abnormal enlargement, tumor
swollen *adj*	being abnormally enlarged
syncope *n*	fainting, brief loss of consciousness
turbid *adj*	cloudy, not clear
umbilicus *n*	the navel, the scar left when the umbilical cord is cut
unmatched blood *n*	blood which can be given to a patient of any blood group
urticarial rash *n*	hives, welts, small white bumps on the skin often caused by insect or plant stings
ward round *n*	a doctor's tour of his patients

Unit 3

aching *adj*	dull, lasting (pain)
aggravating *adj*	making something worse
alleviating *adj*	making something better
auscultation *n*	listening to something, usually with a stethoscope
blunt *adj*	not sharp
cavity *n*	hole, often in a tooth
cyanotic *adj*	blue color of the skin, especially the lips
dull *adj*	not intense (pain)
ECG *n*	electrocardiogram, sometimes known as an EKG
excruciating *adj*	extremely painful
flank *n*	the side of the abdomen
frank *adj*	open, direct, unafraid to say the truth
GAD antibody test *n*	a test to find if there are antibodies to the enzyme GAD
halitosis *n*	bad-smelling breath
lockjaw *n*	involuntary contraction of the jaw muscles
metastasis *n*	(plural **metastases**), secondary cancer growths
mild *adj*	not severe
mucocele *n*	small harmless bluish-colored swelling on the lips or in the mouth
neuropathy *n*	an abnormality in the nervous system
posture *n*	the way the body is held
precipitate *v*	to start, to initiate, to set off
pressing *adj*	a feeling like something is pushing a part of the body
retrosternal *adj*	behind the breastbone
rippling *adj*	like waves on water
sharp *adj*	a sensation like a needle
shooting *adj*	a sensation that travels quickly from one part of the body to another
slight *adj*	not severe
spasm *n*	involuntary contraction of a muscle
stabilize *v*	to use a pin or plate to stop a fractured bone moving
startle response *n*	involuntary reaction to a sudden, unexpected stimulus
suppression *n*	reduction, lowering, decrease
suture *n*	stitch used for sewing a wound
swab *n*	a small piece of cotton used to clean wounds
throbbing *adj*	like a heart beat
tingling *adj*	partially numb, parasthesia, *pins and needles*
trigger *v*	to start, to initiate something
unbearable *adj*	a pain which the patient cannot tolerate

Unit 4

abduction *n*	away from the midline
aneurysm *n*	a pathological swelling in the walls of a blood vessel
anticoagulants *n*	medications used to stop the blood clotting
aphasia *n*	loss of ability to understand or produce language
asymmetry *n*	when one side of something is different from the other
ataxia *n*	lack of coordination
clumsy *adj*	uncoordinated
deficit *n*	a lack of something
diathesis *n*	a hereditary predisposition to an illness

dorsal *adj*	toward the back of the body
drift *n*	the falling movement of a limb when the patient cannot support it
drip line *n*	a tube which carries fluid or medication into the patient's blood
droop *n*	hanging downward
extension *n*	straightening an arm or leg
flexion *n*	bending of a joint so the angle of the bones at the joint decreases
gait *n*	walking
gallop *n*	an abnormal heart sound with three or four separate beats
glenohumeral joint *n*	the shoulder joint
glide *n*	the smooth movement of a joint
grimace *v*	to make an ugly face
harness *n*	tapes or straps used to support some thing
hemorrhagic *adj*	bleeding
INR *n*	a test to measure how quickly the blood clots. Prothrombin Time/International Normalized Ratio
ischemic *adj*	a lack of blood supply to an organ
joint *n*	the place where two bones meet
lesion *n*	a diseased or injured piece of tissue
malformation *n*	a part of the body that is not formed correctly
mobilization *n*	movement
NAD *n*	abbreviation for Nothing Abnormal Detected
neglect *n*	the habit of not using a part of the body that is damaged
neoplasm *n*	an abnormal growth of tissue, a tumor
numbness *n*	lack of physical sensation or feeling
nursing home *n*	an institution for people who cannot look after themselves, usually the elderly
occlude *v*	to block
Partial Thromboplastin Time *n*	
	(aPTT) *n* a test to measure how quickly the blood clots
plasticity *n*	the ability to change shape or function
platelet *n*	a blood cell which takes part in blood clot formation
probe *n*	a sensor that measures something (often electricity)
pronation *n*	to turn the hand so the palm faces down or back
proximal *adj*	near
pucker *v*	to shape the lips as if giving a kiss
puff out *v*	to expand, often used with the cheeks
quadrant *n*	a quarter of a circle
radiocarpal joint *n*	wrist joint
end range *n*	the limit of movement of a joint
rehab *n*	abbreviation for rehabilitation
rub *n*	an abnormal heart sound cause by friction between the pericardium and the heart
set up *v*	to install
shin *n*	the front of the leg below the knee
slurred *adj*	pronounced indistinctly
subarachnoid *adj*	below one of the membranes (arachnoid) that covers the brain
supination *n*	to rotate the hand so the palm faces forwards
temporal *adj*	near temples of skull
thrombus *n*	a blood clot
tourniquet *n*	a piece of equipment (often a rubber tube) to temporarily stop the flow of blood in a limb
UE *n*	upper extremity, arm

Unit 5

biopsy *n*	removal and examination of example of tissue from a living body for diagnostic purposes
bruising *n*	a blue coloring of the skin caused by injury
carcinoma *n*	invasive malignant tumor that tends to metastasize to other areas of the body
CVS *n*	abbreviation for Cardiovascular system
debris *n*	unwanted, waste material, e.g. wax in the ear
degenerative disease *n*	
	a disorder in which the patient slowly gets worse or deteriorates

derangement *n*	an abnormality in the usual arrangement
erupted *adj*	visible
erythematous *adj*	reddening of the skin caused by dilatation and congestion of the capillaries
excision biopsy *n*	the complete removal of a lesion for microscopic examination
external auditory meatus *n*	
	the canal that leads from the external ear to the ear drum
exudate *n*	fluid, especially lymph or blood, that escapes from a wound or lesion
febrile *adj*	characterized by fever, feverish
floss *v*	to clean between the teeth with a thread
gauze pad *n*	an absorbent piece of cotton
gingiva *n*	the gums
gingival recession *n*	receding or shrinking of the gums
gingivitis *n*	inflammation of the gums
ice pack *n*	a cloth bag contain ice which is placed against a wound used to reduce swelling
jaw *n*	the bone to which the lower teeth are attached
ligament *n*	sheet or band of tough, fibrous tissue connecting bones or cartilages at a joint or supporting an organ
lymph node *n*	small gland which is part of the lymphatic system
lymphadenopathy *n*	a chronic, abnormal enlargement of the lymph nodes, usually associated with disease
mandible *n*	lower jaw
mastication *n*	chewing
meatus *n*	a body opening or passage
mucosa *n*	the lining of the internal surfaces of the body
NSAIDs *n*	Non-Steroid Anti-Inflammatory Drugs
occlusion *n*	*(dental)* the manner in which the upper and lower teeth meet
otalgia *n*	earache
palpate *v*	to feel
papilla *n*	the piece of gum between the teeth
pericoronal *adj*	around the crown of a tooth
periodontal ligament *n*	the fibers that connect the teeth to the bone
periodontitis *n*	inflammation of the fibers that connect the teeth to the jaws
pocket *n*	an abnormal recess between the gums and the tooth
puff *n*	short, forceful exhalation of breath
radiolucency *n*	allowing the passage of x-rays or other radiation
side effect *n*	the additional, sometimes unwanted effect of an action
sinusitis *n*	inflammation of the nasal sinuses
socket *n*	the hole left in the jaw after a tooth has been extracted
spatula *n*	a flat instrument for holding down the tongue
temperomandibular joint *n*	
	the jaw joint, the joint between the mandible and the cranium
tenderness *n*	sensitivity to pain
third molar *n*	wisdom teeth, the last molar teeth
tinnitus *n*	a hissing or ringing sound in the ear
TMJ *n*	temperomandibular joint
unevenness *n*	lack of uniformity, consistency
wisdom tooth *n*	the last molar
withdrawal symptoms *n*	
	the unpleasant feeling a person has when an addictive drug, e.g., nicotine is taken away

Audio Script

Lesson 1

Page 3, Exercise H

CD T-2

Dr. Murray: Come in, please. It's Mrs. Thurston and this is Mark, isn't it?

Mrs. Thurston: That's right, Dr. Murray.

Dr. Murray: Can I introduce a colleague? This is Robert Mitchell. He's a medical student.

Robert: Nice to meet you.

Mrs. Thurston: Nice to meet you, too.

Dr. Murray: Now, how can we help you?

Mrs. Thurston: Yes, well the problem is Mark. I know he's at a difficult age and all teenagers just want to drink soda and eat junk food, but he drinks like about three bottles of soda a day. Those big bottles! And then of course, he's always going to the bathroom. You know sometimes I think . . .

Dr. Murray: OK, thank you, Mrs. Thurston. Can I just ask Mark a few questions? OK, Mark, so you've been feeling very thirsty . . .

Page 3, Exercise I

CD T-3

Dr. Murray: When did this thirstiness begin?

Mark: I'd say about two or three weeks ago.

Dr. Murray: And are you thirsty all the time?

Mark: Yes. But especially after I have eaten.

Dr. Murray: And how often do you have to go to the bathroom?

Mark: Oh, I don't know. About six times a day. Maybe more.

Dr. Murray: What about at night?

Mark: Yeah, I have to get up in the night as well.

Dr. Murray: Have you had any problems like this before, Mark?

Mark: No, I don't think so.

Dr. Murray: OK, Mark. You're doing great. Now, are you having any other problems?

Mark: Like what?

Dr. Murray: Well, other health problems, school, you know- anything?

Mrs. Thurston: His teachers say he's lazy. Just won't work.

Dr. Murray: Mark?

Mark: Well, I'm always tired. I used to play a lot of basketball, but now I get tired in no time.

Dr. Murray: And when did this start?

Mark: About a month ago, I guess.

Dr. Murray: Anything else?

Mark: No, I don't think so.

Dr. Murray: Robert, are there any questions that you would like to ask Mark?

Robert: Thank you, Doctor. Yes, there are. Mark, have you been losing weight recently?

Mark: No, I don't think so. Don't really know.

Mrs. Thurston: Actually doctor, it's funny you should say that, but I was saying to his dad the other day that Mark's looking thin. But his dad said that it was just a stage he was going through and that he would fill out later.

Robert: Thank you. Just one more question, Mrs. Thurston. Has anyone else in your family had a similar problem?

Mrs. Thurston: No, I don't think so. My mother died of a stroke and my father is still alive, but he's not well. You know, he has problems with his heart. And he has problems with his eyes as well—nothing like Mark has.

Robert: Thank you very much, Mrs. Thurston.

Lesson 3

Page 6, Exercise B

CD T-4

Dr. Murray: Now, Mark, I'd just like to check out a few things. Could you take off your shoes, socks, and shirt, please? OK, that's fine. And now could you stand on the scales and we'll measure your height and weight. OK, Robert, so Mark weighs 110 lbs and is 5 feet 6 inches tall.

OK, Mark, now I'm just going to take your temperature. Open wide. Fine. While we're waiting for that, I'll take your blood pressure.

OK, so your temperature is 98.6 degrees and your blood pressure is 120 over 70. No problem there. Let's check your pulse.

OK, Robert. Heart rate of 60 and respiration rate of 15.

Fine, Mark. You're doing great. Now, if you could just stand up and I'll have a look at your eyes and ears. Open your mouth please. Say aaah. OK, Robert.

Everything OK there.

Now, if you could just turn around and look up to the ceiling, I'd like to check your neck. Robert, would you make a note that there is a slight swelling of the thyroid gland.

Now, . . .

Lesson 4

Page 9, Exercise D

CD
T-5

Dr. Murray: Good morning.

Mrs. Thurston and Mark: Good morning.

Dr. Murray: So, Mark, How are you feeling?

Mark: Pretty much the same, Doctor.

Dr. Murray: OK. Well, Mark, we have the lab results and as we suspected, it appears that you have diabetes.

Mrs. Thurston: Oh, no! That's what my father has. Does this mean that Mark will have to give himself injections? And my dad has all these other problems that they say come from diabetes.

Dr. Murray: Don't worry too much, Mrs. Thurston. Each case is different and we have made a lot of progress in the last few years.

Mark: Does this mean I won't be able to play sports anymore?

Dr. Murray: Not at all, Mark. You will be able to lead a completely normal life. You can eat more or less the same food as all your friends. No one will even know you have diabetes.

Mrs. Thurston: But he'll have to give himself injections, won't he?

Dr. Murray: Not necessarily. There are some new gadgets that you wear that do away with injections.

Mark: Yeah, there's another kid at school who has one of those. But he has to take blood samples.

Dr. Murray: Yes, that's right, you have to check the amount of sugar in your blood.

Mrs. Thurston: Don't worry, Mark. I'm sure everything is going to be OK.

Dr. Murray: That's right. Thank you, Mrs. Thurston. But please remember, Mark, diabetes is a serious condition and it can have long-term consequences if you don't follow a very careful treatment plan. OK? Now, let's go through everything step by step.

Lesson 5

Page 10, Exercise C

CD
T-6

Nutritionist: Hello, it's Mrs. Thurston and Mark, isn't it?

Mrs. Thurston: That's right. We're here about Mark's diet.

Nutritionist: Yes, Dr. Murray asked me to speak to you. I expect that he's explained all about diabetes and how we treat it.

Mrs. Thurston: Yes, he has, but I'm still not sure exactly what I have to cook for Mark. Is it going to be a lot of trouble?

Nutritionist: Don't worry. Mark will be able to eat more or less the same as the rest of the family. We just have to make sure he is getting the right amount of food at the right time and he has a balanced diet. Simple!

Mrs. Thurston: Well, I hope so!

Nutritionist: OK, Mark. First we need to calculate how many calories you need per day. I've got your age, height and weight here in your notes, but I also need to know whether you are especially active. I mean, do you play a lot of sports?

Mark: Yes, I would say so. I used to play basketball every day before I got sick.

Nutritionist: OK, so let me see. According to the computer, …..you are going to need about 2250 calories per day.

Mrs. Thurston: What does that mean?

Nutritionist: OK, Mrs. Thurston, we're coming to that. Mark, do you know what carbohydrates are?

Mark: Sure, that's where you get your energy from. Things like bread and potatoes.

Nutritionist: Right! And what about nutrition labels, can you understand them?

Mark: Sure. They tell you how many calories you get from one serving and how much protein and vitamins there are. Can I ask you a question though?

Nutritionist: Sure, fire away!

Mark: I don't really get this thing about servings. I'm used to my mom's servings, and then you go to a restaurant and they give you tiny little servings. It seems all servings are different. How can you know how many calories you're getting?

Nutritionist: You're exactly right. The trick is to look at the nutrition label carefully. It always says how many ounces or grams there are in a regular serving.

Mark: So, if I weigh one of mom's regular servings, I'll be able to tell how many calories I'm getting.

Nutritionist: Do you think you can do that?

Mark: No problem.

Nutritionist: OK. Now there are a few more things you need to know. First, some foods don't have nutrition labels, like potatoes, so I'm going to give you a chart with that information. Next, the way you cook the food affects the number of calories per serving. Fried rice has much more energy than boiled rice for example.

Mark: OK. So I weigh one of mom's monster servings, look up the calories on the chart and then calculate how many calories there are in one serving. Easy!

Nutritionist: Oh, there's one last thing. You have to make sure you eat a balanced diet.

Mark: That's the food pyramid thing, isn't it?

Nutritionist: You got it! As a rough guide, 50% of your diet should be carbohydrate, 25% fruit and vegetables and 25% protein.

Mark: So no fatty things and candy?

Nutritionist: Keep them to a minimum. You can eat them, but just don't eat too many.

Lesson 6

Page 12, Exercise C

CD
T-7

Dr. Murray: OK, Mark. We need to do a couple of tests. The first one is your thyroid function test.

Mark: What's that? I think you told me last time but I've forgotten. There was so much to understand.

Dr. Murray: It tests how well your thyroid is working. We think it's working a bit too well and we want to check. Clear? Any questions?

Mark: I'm sorry. What's my thyroid?

Dr. Murray: OK, let's start from the beginning. Your thyroid gland, in some ways, is like the accelerator on a car. It controls, how fast your system works and lots of other things as well. The thyroid gland produces a hormone, that's a chemical messenger, called thyroxin. If there is too much in your blood, your system goes too quickly, if there isn't enough it goes too slowly. Do you follow?

Mark: Sure.

Dr. Murray: So if the thyroid gland is like the accelerator, what is thyroxin like?

Mark: Erm, Well I suppose it's like the gas. Too much and you go too fast.

Dr. Murray: You got it!

Mark: But what has this got to do with my diabetes?

Dr. Murray: Well, you remember last time I told you that carbohydrate makes your blood sugar go up and insulin and exercise keep your blood sugar levels down . . .

Mark: Sure, that's why I have to reduce my insulin if I do a lot of exercise.

Dr. Murray: Right! And you've been having problems balancing the two, haven't you?

Mark: Yes, it's not easy, but I'm trying.

Dr. Murray: Well, this is where the thyroid comes in. It's really difficult to keep your blood sugar right if your thyroid gland keeps putting its foot on the accelerator.

Mark: And I'm trying to put my foot on the brake at the same time.

Dr. Murray: OK! So you see why we have to keep checking your thyroid function.

Mark: Yes, that's much clearer.

Dr. Murray: OK, Mark, I'm sure you understood but just to check, can you run through it again for me.

Mark: OK, my thyroid function tests are high, but only by a bit. So we want to . . .

Unit 2 Working under pressure

Lesson 1

Page 16, Exercise B

CD
T-8

Robert: Good morning, Dr. Tan. I'm Robert Mitchell. I'll be with you for the next month.

Jenny: Hi, Robert. That's right, Dr. Murray told me you would be coming. And by the way, we don't have time for Dr. Tan in here. This is life in the fast lane. Just call me Jenny.

Robert: OK, Jenny. Looking forward to working with you.

Jenny: Me, too.

Robert: Jenny, I've never worked in the Emergency Room before. Is there any advice you could give me?

Jenny: Sure. Number one: Don't panic. Keep cool.

Robert: OK, easy to say, but difficult to do.

Jenny: Right! Then, if you are not sure, ask. This is really important. I've been doing this job for six years and I'm still learning.

Robert: OK.

Jenny: Life in the ER is exhausting. You work long hours, you're on your feet all the time and the pressure can get to you. So, my advice is get plenty of sleep when you can. You'll need it.

Robert: So, no partying after work.

Jenny: You'll be so tired, you won't even be able to switch on the TV.

Robert: Sounds fun!

Jenny: And finally, never use the "Q" word.

Robert: Excuse me?

Jenny: Never say, "Things are real quiet today." It is guaranteed to bring in ten ambulances and three helicopters.

Robert: Gotcha!

Jenny: OK, so let's go. I've just had a look at this patient and I've sent him for a scan. While we're waiting for the results, please get a nurse to contact the next of kin and arrange for the dental intern to examine the patient. I have a feeling that he has a fractured jaw.

Page 17, Exercise C

CD T-9

Robert: Hello, is that Doctor Plantz?

Dr. Plantz: Speaking.

Robert: Good morning, doctor. This is Robert Mitchell from ER.

Dr. Plantz: Morning, Robert. What can I do for you?

Robert: We have a patient here with head injuries and a possible mandibular fracture. Could you come down and take a look?

Dr. Plantz: Sure, but I'm just finishing a ward round. Is the patient stabilized?

Robert: Sorry, I missed that. What did you say? Sterilized?

Dr. Plantz: No stabilized! I mean, can you wait about a quarter of an hour?

Robert: About fifteen minutes. Sure. Bye.

Lesson 2

Page 18, Exercise A

CD T-10

Nurse: It's Mr. Slenkovich, Wayne's father, isn't it?

Mr. Slenkovich: That's right. What's happened to Wayne? Is he all right?

Nurse: He'll be fine, Mr. Slenkovich. But first things first. It seems that Wayne finished work at 8 o'clock in the evening and was just leaving the store when two men attacked him.

Mr. Slenkovich: Had he already been to the bank with the money from the store?

Nurse: I'm really not sure. Anyway, some people saw the assault and called an ambulance. The paramedics checked Wayne over, put on a neck brace, and brought him in.

Mr. Slenkovich: Did they get the guys who attacked him?

Nurse: I don't know but the police have already spoken to Wayne. Dr. Tan examined him when he arrived and sent him to have a scan. He had a dislocated jaw, which we put back in place, but there don't seem to be any broken bones. Anyway, we decided to keep him in for the night.

Mr. Slenkovich: Why? If he's OK, why can't he come home?

Nurse: Well he was knocked out for about ten minutes after the attack and the doctor thinks that it is best to keep an eye on him.

Mr. Slenkovich: Can I see him?

Nurse: Just for a minute. He needs to rest.

Page 19, Exercise D

CD T-11

Nurse: Good news, Wayne. The doctor says you can go home now.

Wayne: Great!

Nurse: But before you leave, can I just check on a few things?

Wayne: Sure.

Nurse: The doctor would like you to take these pills. You have to take one pill every eight hours until they are all finished. There is enough for a week. OK?

Wayne: OK. So one when I get up, one at lunchtime, and one before I go to bed.

Nurse: Right. Now, Dr. Tan says you have a mild concussion and so you must not drive for at least a week.

Wayne: No problem. I don't really feel like driving at the moment.

Nurse: OK, now your jaw. You mustn't open your mouth wide for a few days.

Wayne: What if I have to yawn?

Nurse: Good point. If you support your jaw with your hands, it should help

Wayne: OK.

Lesson 3

Page 20, Exercise B

CD T-12

Robert: OK, it's Mrs. Legrange, isn't it? I believe your husband collapsed at home. Can you tell me what happened?

Mrs. Legrange: Yes, Doctor, we had just gotten back to the house, and Chuck was complaining that he wasn't feeling well, and that he had heartburn and was sort of itchy and then he sort of went funny and fainted.

Robert: Has he had any problems like this before? Fainting or heartburn or anything?

Mrs. Legrange: No, I don't think so.

Robert: Is he taking any medication at the moment?

Mrs. Legrange: He has low blood pressure and he's taking some little yellow pills.

Robert: Had he eaten anything before he passed out?

Mrs. Legrange: Oh, yes. We had just had lunch with our daughter.

Robert: What did you have for lunch?

Mrs. Legrange: We had oysters. It was her birthday.

Robert: Is Mr. Legrange allergic to seafood?

Mrs. Legrange: I'm not sure. We almost never eat seafood. I don't like it much.

Robert: OK. Did Mr. Legrange fall or bang his head before he passed out?

Mrs. Legrange: No. Like I said, we had just come in and he came over all funny . . .

Lesson 4

Page 22, Exercise B

CD
T-13

Robert: Good evening. It's Mrs. Tolan, isn't it?

Mrs. Tolan: That's right. What do you think is wrong with Louise?

Robert: Well she's in no immediate danger, so I'd like to ask you a few questions before I check her over. Now, you say that she is having problems breathing and she's wheezing.

Mrs. Tolan: That's right.

Robert: When did this start?

Mrs. Tolan: Well, she has had a bit of a cold since yesterday, but she got really bad during the night.

Robert: Has she had attacks like this before?

Mrs. Tolan: She's had colds, of course, but nothing like this.

Robert: Does she have a cough as well?

Mrs. Tolan: Yes. A bit.

Robert: Is it a loud cough?

Mrs. Tolan: No, not really.

Robert: Has she vomited at all?

Mrs. Tolan: No. Actually she wouldn't eat anything all day. She's really lost her appetite.

Robert: Has she been drinking anything?

Mrs. Tolan: She had some milk before she went to bed, but not much.

Robert: Do you remember if she had choked on anything, like a toy, before the wheezing started?

Mrs. Tolan: No, I don't think so. It just started when she went to bed.

Robert: Has Louise had any other medical problems?

Mrs. Tolan: Well she had measles last year.

Robert: Anything else?

Mrs. Tolan: No, just colds and things.

Robert: Does anyone else in the family have chest problems?

Mrs. Tolan: No, we're all in good health.

Robert: And her grandparents?

Mrs. Tolan: No, they're fine as well.

Lesson 5

Page 24, Exercise A

CD
T-14

Robert: Good afternoon, Susan. OK, I see from your notes that you have a fever and a headache.

Susan: That's right.

Robert: And when did all this begin?

Susan: About two days ago. I woke up feeling tired and I didn't feel like eating. Then during the day I was sort of hot and cold and started sweating. So, I thought OK it's a cold and I'll call in sick. But then last night I started

with this really bad headache. I've never had a headache like this before. Really painful. And then today I started having problems with my eyes. That's why I'm wearing the sunglasses. It seems like my eyes are really sensitive to the sun. And I don't know why, but I have a stiff neck. I must have slept in a strange position and hurt my neck. Anyway, I decided this was more than a cold and came in here.

Robert: You did the right thing. It's definitely more than a cold. Can I just ask you a couple of questions about the headache? You say it began about 24 hours ago?

Susan: That's right.

Robert: Where is the headache? Front? Back?

Susan: At the front.

Robert: One side or both?

Susan: Both.

Robert: OK, I think we will have to do a few more investigations. I'm going to call the doctor and then I think we will have to do a lumbar puncture. The nurse will stay with you and explain everything.

Unit 3 Breaking bad news

Lesson 2

Page 32, Exercise A

CD
T-15

1. You should have called me.
   You should have called me.

2. Why didn't you come sooner?
   Why didn't you come sooner?

3. Sorry, what did you say?
   Sorry, what did you say?

4. Did you understand what I said?
   Did you understand what I said?

5. How many times have you been here?
   How many times have you been here?

6. Why didn't you finish the treatment?
   Why didn't you finish the treatment?

Page 32, Exercise B

CD
T-16

1. You should have called me.
   You should have called me.

2. Why didn't you come sooner?
   Why didn't you come sooner?

3. Sorry, what did you say?
   Sorry, what did you say?

4. Did you understand what I said?
   Did you understand what I said?

5. How many times have you been here?

How many times have you been here?

6. Why didn't you finish the treatment?
   Why didn't you finish the treatment?

Page 32, Exercise C

CD
T-17

1. Why didn't you let me know sooner?
2. Are you telling me everything?
3. Sorry, can you say that again?
4. I don't think I need to see you again.
5. What do you mean by that?
6. And don't forget to bring the urine sample.
7. I don't think there's anything wrong with you.
8. Why didn't you call me?

Page 32, Exercise D

CD
T-18

Dr. Murray: Good morning, Mr. Bloom. How's it going?

Mr. Bloom: Not very well, I'm afraid.

Dr. Murray: Well, let's see. Last time you were here, when was it-two months ago-you were having problems with your back.

Mr. Bloom: That's right. And it seems to be getting worse.

Dr. Murray: Oh dear. Why didn't you call me sooner?

Mr. Bloom: I was hoping it would get better.

Dr. Murray: Well, let's go over your symptoms again, shall we? Exactly where does it hurt?

Mr. Bloom: Mmm, at the bottom of my back but it sometimes goes up to my shoulders as well.

Dr. Murray: Can you describe the pain?

Mr. Bloom: Well, it's sort of a cramp. It seems like the muscles are all tense and stiff.

Dr. Murray: How bad is the pain?

Mr. Bloom: Well, sometimes it's really bad. I had to take a couple of days off work last week because it was so bad.

Dr. Murray: And how long do these cramps last?

Mr. Bloom: It seems to vary. Sometimes a couple of hours, sometimes less.

Dr. Murray: Does it hurt at any particular time of day?

Mr. Bloom: It's bad in the morning. I'm really stiff when I get up.

Dr. Murray: And does anything trigger the pain, you know, anything that brings it on, makes it start?

Mr. Bloom: I know this is going to sound funny, but if I'm worried or nervous about something or if things go wrong at work, it seems to come on.

Dr. Murray: Robert, do you have any questions for Mr. Bloom?

Robert: Well, just a couple. Mr. Bloom, does anything make the pain get better?

Mr. Bloom: Well, I've noticed that if I take a nap, it goes away.

Robert: Right! And does anything make it worse, like bending or working in the garden?

Mr. Bloom: No, not really. Just the stress.

Robert: Have you had anything like this before?

Mr. Bloom: No, I don't think so. I hurt my back gardening once, but that was years ago.

Robert: Has anyone in your family had anything like this?

Mr. Bloom: No, not as far as I know.

Robert: I see from your notes that you are an engineer. Does this mean you have to do lots of physical work?

Mr. Bloom: No, actually most of my work is sitting at a computer.

Robert: Well, I think that's all. Thank you, Mr. Bloom.

Dr. Murray: OK, I think we ought to take some X-rays to see if we can see anything. If you see the receptionist, she will make an appointment. Thank you very much, Mr. Bloom.

Mr. Bloom: There's just one more thing. You know, I've been feeling a bit depressed lately.

Dr. Murray: OK. Tell me about it. When did you start to feel depressed…?

Page 33, Exercise E

CD
T-19

Dr. Murray: Good morning, Mr. Bloom. How's it going?

Mr. Bloom: Not very well, I'm afraid.

Dr. Murray: Well, let's see. Last time you were here, when was it-two months ago-you were having problems with your back.

Mr. Bloom: That's right. And it seems to be getting worse.

Dr. Murray: Oh dear. Why didn't you call me sooner?

Mr. Bloom: I was hoping it would get better.

Dr. Murray: Well, let's go over your symptoms again, shall we? Exactly where does it hurt?

Mr. Bloom: Mmm, at the bottom of my back but it sometimes goes up to my shoulders as well.

Dr. Murray: Can you describe the pain?

Mr. Bloom: Well, it's sort of a cramp. It seems like the muscles are all tense and stiff.

Dr. Murray: How bad is the pain?

Mr. Bloom: Well, sometimes it's really bad. I had to take a couple of days off work last week because it was so bad.

Dr. Murray: And how long do these cramps last?

Mr. Bloom: It seems to vary. Sometimes a couple of hours, sometimes less.

Dr. Murray: Does it hurt at any particular time of day?

Mr. Bloom: It's bad in the morning. I'm really stiff when I get up.

Dr. Murray: And does anything trigger the pain, you know, anything that brings it on, makes it start?

Mr. Bloom: I know this is going to sound funny but if I'm worried or nervous about something or if things go wrong at work, it seems to come on.

Dr. Murray: Robert, do you have any questions for Mr. Bloom?

Robert: Well, just a couple. Mr. Bloom, does anything make the pain get better?

Mr. Bloom: Well, I've noticed that if I take a nap, it goes away.

Robert: Right! And does anything make it worse, like bending or working in the garden?

Mr. Bloom: No, not really. Just the stress.

Robert: Have you had anything like this before?

Mr. Bloom: No, I don't think so. I hurt my back gardening once, but that was years ago.

Robert: Has anyone in your family had anything like this?

Mr. Bloom: No, not as far as I know.

Robert: I see from your notes that you are an engineer. Does this mean you have to do lots of physical work?

Mr. Bloom: No, actually most of my work is sitting at a computer.

Robert: Well, I think that's all. Thank you, Mr. Bloom.

Dr. Murray: OK, I think we ought to take some X-rays to see if we can see anything. If you see the receptionist, she will make an appointment. Thank you very much, Mr. Bloom.

Mr. Bloom: There's just one more thing. You know, I've been feeling a bit depressed lately.

Dr. Murray: OK. Tell me about it. When did you start to feel depressed . . .?

Lesson 3

Page 35, Exercise D

CD T-20

1. Mr. Bloom's next, isn't he?
   Mr. Bloom's next, isn't he?

2. You've got Mr. Bloom's notes, haven't you?
   You've got Mr. Bloom's notes, haven't you?

3. You're here for a chest X-ray, aren't you?
   You're here for a chest X-ray, aren't you?

4. This isn't going to hurt, is it?
   This isn't going to hurt, is it?

5. I can leave now, can't I?
   I can leave now, can't I?

Page 35, Exercise E

CD T-21

1. Mr. Bloom's next, isn't he?
   Mr. Bloom's next, isn't he?

2. You've got Mr. Bloom's notes, haven't you?
   You've got Mr. Bloom's notes, haven't you?

3. You're here for a chest X-ray, aren't you?
   You're here for a chest X-ray, aren't you?

4. This isn't going to hurt, is it?
   This isn't going to hurt, is it?

CD T-22

5. I can leave now, can't I?
   I can leave now, can't I?

Lesson 4

Page 36 Exercise B

Dr. Murray: So, Robert, let's go over Mr. Bloom's case. Can you review it for me?

Robert: Sure. The patient presented on February 4 this year complaining of lower back pain. There was no history of trauma. Analgesics were prescribed and the patient was advised to avoid strenuous work and heavy lifting.

Dr. Murray: Go on.

Robert: The patient was seen again on April 6 complaining that he was still in pain and that the condition was worse. He also complained of depression. The patient was referred for radiography.

Dr. Murray: OK. Let's have a look at the radiograph. What do you think?

Robert: Let me see. Well, it looks fine to me.

Dr. Murray: To me, too. So what do you suggest?

Robert: Well, I think he should be referred for a psychological evaluation at this point. Maybe the back pain is psychosomatic. After all, he seems to be rather depressed.

Dr. Murray: All right. That might be valuable but I also think he ought to be referred to a neurologist.

Lesson 5

Page 38, Exercise A

CD T-23

Dr. Murray: OK, we've got the neurologist's report now. But before I show it to you, I asked you to do a bit of research about Mr. Bloom's case. What did you come up with?.

Robert: Well, I started off by investigating all the possible causes of muscle spasms in the back and legs in a middle-aged patient.

Dr. Murray: And?

Robert: Well, as you can imagine, there are lots, but I think I have narrowed it down to four possible conditions. First, there is a possibility that it is chronic tetanus. Mr. Bloom is a keen gardener, and it is possible that he has become infected from the soil. He has stiffness of the neck, which is typical of tetanus, but he has no spasms of the jaw muscles, and 75% of patients present with lockjaw.

Dr. Murray: OK, but what about the depression? Is depression a common symptom of tetanus?

Robert: Not as far as I know. However, there is a very rare condition known as Stiff Person Syndrome where depression is very commonly associated with stiffness and spasms in the back and lower limbs.

Dr. Murray: Tell me more.

Robert: Well it seems that the spasms happen when the patient gets some strong emotional stimulus, such as when they are surprised or angry.

Dr. Murray: And how would you confirm diagnosis?

Robert: There is a blood test, but not all patients with the clinical signs and symptoms test positive.

Dr. Murray: OK. Anything else?

Robert: Well there is another very rare condition called Isaac's Syndrome, which is characterized by painful muscles spasms.

Dr. Murray: And how is it different from Stiff Person Syndrome?

Robert: Well, the big difference is that the spasms don't stop when the patient is asleep— in Stiff Person Syndrome, they do.

Dr. Murray: Well, that should be easy to check. And what's the last one?

Robert: There is the possibility of Multiple Sclerosis. Painful muscles spasms are common and depression is reported in many patients.

Dr. Murray: But there would be other symptoms as well, wouldn't there?

Robert: Yes, patients often complain of paresthesia or "pins and needles" and fatigue is very common.

Dr. Murray: OK, Robert. You've done a good job there.

Unit 4 Calling in the Stroke Team

Lesson 1

Page 45, Exercise D

CD T-24

Dr. Oliveira: Good morning, is that the stroke unit?

Woman: That's right. What can we do for you?

Dr. Oliveira: We have a patient who has just come in and we suspect she has had a stroke. Can I speak to a doctor, please?

Woman: Putting you through.

Male: Good morning, Steve Harbinger speaking.

Dr. Oliveira: Good morning, Dr. Harbinger, this is Luciana Oliveira from Primary Care. We have a patient over here that we think might have had a stroke.

Dr. Harbinger: OK, can you run through the case?

Dr. Oliveira: Sure. The patient's name is Linda Marshall. She is a 62-year-old, retired factory worker who lives with her husband. She has a history of ischemic heart disease although we are still trying to get the details. Her husband reports that she complained about chest pain this morning and then shortly after developed right sided hemiparesis with mild dysarthria.

Dr. Harbinger: OK, let me get that right, Chest pains and then right-sided weakness with speech difficulty?

Dr. Oliveira: That's right. Vital signs OK. BP 144 over 87, Pulse 89, Respiratory rate 20 and temperature of 98.6.

Dr. Harbinger: When did she have the attack?

Dr. Oliveira: At about 9.00 this morning.

Dr. Harbinger: About two hours ago. OK. Sounds like a possible candidate for thrombolytics. Send her for a CT scan, do a 12 lead ECG, we need international normalized ratio (INR) and activated partial thromboplastin time (aPTT). And find out what you can about the heart disease. I'm on my way.

Dr. Oliveira: Wow! Superdoc or what!

Lesson 3

Page 48, Exercise B

CD T-25

Robert: Hi, is that Dr. Kim?

Dr. Kim: Speaking.

Robert: Good morning, Dr. Kim. This is Robert Mitchell speaking from Ashville Hospital. We have a patient here whom you treated about 10 days ago. She has presented with a stroke and we would like to check up on the treatment she had with you.

Dr. Kim: Sure. What's the patient's name?

Robert: Mrs. Linda Marshall, aged 62.

Dr. Kim: OK, let me check the computer. OK, here we are. Retired factory worker. Right?

Robert: Right.

Dr. Kim: OK, she presented with retrosternal chest pain. The electrocardiogram showed ST segment and T wave abnormality but there was no Q wave abnormality. A diagnosis of non-transmural MI was made and the patient was admitted.

Robert: OK, let me just write that down. Retrosternal chest pain. ECG, no Q wave abnormality but ST segment and T wave abnormality. Diagnosis: myocardial infarction. OK.

Dr. Kim: Right. We gave her the usual acute MI medications: IV morphine, aspirin, nitroglycerin, and heparin and put her under observation.

Robert: OK, so we have intra venous morphine, aspirin, nitroglycerin, and heparin. OK.

Dr. Kim: She responded very well and after six hours her T waves were looking much better. We ran a CK-MB myocardial enzyme test, which was elevated and confirmed the diagnosis.

Robert: CK-MB high.

Dr. Kim: After 24 hours, ECG was almost normal and, as you would expect CK-MB levels were still high. The pain had subsided and then, against our advice, the patient discharged herself! She said she was on holiday and wanted to spend time with her grandchildren, not with a bunch of doctors, if I remember her words correctly.

Robert: Wow, so she just walked right out of the hospital. No medication. Nothing?

Dr. Kim: That's right. She signed her own discharge forms and off she went.

Robert: Thanks for the tip. Dr. Kim, we are considering giving her thrombolytics. Was there anything in her treatment or history to contraindicate thrombolytics?

Dr. Kim: Like I said, she's not on anticoagulants, but it would be a good idea to do another ECG and an INR.

Robert: Yes, that's what we were planning. Thanks again, Dr. Kim. Good to talk to you.

Dr. Kim: You're welcome, Robert. Hope the case goes well.

Lesson 4

Page 50, Exercise B

CD T-26

Dr. Harbinger: OK, Robert, what have you got for me? Dr. Oliveira gave me some of the facts, but it'll be good practice for you to review the case.

Robert: OK, this is Mrs. Marshall, a 62-year-old retired factory worker. She was treated for a myocardial infarct ten days ago in California where she was admitted and received morphine, aspirin, nitroglycerin, heparin. She then discharged herself after 36 hours.

Dr. Harbinger: What! She just walked out?

Robert: Said she wanted to spend her holidays with her grandchildren, not with a bunch of doctors!

Dr. Harbinger: Well, she has a point I suppose. OK, what next?

Robert: She presented here at 10.00 a.m. She had mild disarthria and her husband reported that she had complained of chest pains at about 9.00 a.m. and later developed hemiplegia on the right. Her vital signs were as follows: Blood pressure: 144/87. Heart rate: 89. Respiratory Rate: 20. Temperature: 98.6ºF. On examination, she had a NIH stroke scale of 9.

Dr. Harbinger: NIH 9.OK, now what else have you got for me in the way of . . .

Page 50, Exercise C

CD T-27

Dr. Harbinger: OK, so we first have to decide if we can use thrombolytics. What do you think, Robert?

Robert: OK, let me give you the important physical signs first. Her heart seems fine: there are no murmurs, rubs, or gallops.

Dr. Harbinger: OK. So there are no signs of pericarditis. That's good.

Robert: She seems to be alert but has mild expressive dysphasia. She has a mild facial droop on the right and there is a profound deficit in her right field of vision. She has drift in both right limbs and there is also some sensory loss.

Dr. Harbinger: OK, so far.

Robert: OK. Now the lab results. Glucose was 122 milligrams per deciliter.

Dr. Harbinger: 122, that's OK. It's within normal limits.

Robert: No problems with coagulation. The INR is 1.2.

Dr. Harbinger: 1.2 sounds good to me.

Robert: Platelets are 93000.

Dr. Harbinger: 93K is OK. And we have the CT scan?

Robert: Here it is. The report reads, "No acute hemorrhagic infarct or subarachnoid blood. No evidence of intracranial neoplasm, arteriovenous malformation, or aneurysm."

Dr. Harbinger: OK. And the ECG?

Robert: Absence of R waves, which indicates a previous myocardial infarct.

Unit 5 Referring a patient

Lesson 3
Page 62, Exercise A

CD T-28

Upper right eight, clear
seven occlusal
six MO
five DO
four absent
three, two and one clear

Upper left one, two, three clear
four occlusal
five MO
six MOD
seven and eight clear

Lower right eight absent
seven MOD
six MOD

five occlusal

four, three, two, one clear

Lower left one, two, three, four, clear

five DO

six MO

seven clear

eight absent

 Page 62, Exercise B

CD T-29

Dr. Hoffer: Good morning, is that Dr. Murray's office?

Secretary: Yes, it is, Can I help you?

Dr. Hoffer: Yes, this is Dr. Hoffer. Is it possible to speak to Dr. Murray?

Secretary: Yes, you're lucky. He's right here in the office. Just a moment.

Dr. Murray: Hi, David, how's it going?

Dr. Hoffer: Fine thanks, Bruce. I was just phoning about the case you sent me last week-Lucia Moreno.

Dr. Murray: That's right. The patient with the earache. What did you find?

Dr. Hoffer: Well, you were right about the impacted lower right eight. There is marked pericoronal inflammation and the radiograph shows there is some radiolucency around the root. I suspect there is a chronic abscess.

Dr. Murray: So, what do you think? Should it be extracted?

Dr. Hoffer: No question. However, I think that it will need surgical extraction, even though the crown is visible, it is badly impacted.

Dr. Murray: OK. Can you arrange that?

Dr. Hoffer: Sure. The lower left eight is also impacted, so I'll do both at the same time.

Dr. Murray: And what about the TMJ? What do you think?

Dr. Hoffer: These TMJs are always tricky. I agree there is a small click and also the patient can only open her mouth about 30mm, which is less than normal.

Dr. Murray: Yes, I noticed that.

Dr. Hoffer: Is the patient under a lot of stress at the moment?

Dr. Murray: Well, she's just finishing her Master's, so I imagine she is.

Dr. Hoffer: Well, let's just start her on benzodiazepines and something like aspirin and see how it goes. Bruce, there was just one other thing. I noticed a small erythematous lesion on the floor of the mouth. It might not be anything but I think we should do a biopsy, just in case.

Dr. Murray: Ooops. I missed that. Yes, sounds like a good idea. I've seen one or two otalgias caused by tumors in the floor of the mouth.

Dr. Hoffer: So, from a dental point of view, we have three possible causes of the otalgia: the impacted eight, the TMJ and the tumor on the floor of the mouth.

Dr. Murray: OK, David, can I leave the treatment with you?

Dr. Hoffer: No problem.

Dr. Murray: Thanks a lot, David. And one more thing, would you mind putting that in writing for the files?

Dr. Hoffer: Sure thing, Bruce. You can't be too careful these days with all these lawyers around. I'll get it off today.

Dr. Murray: Thanks, David. See you around.

Dr. Hoffer: See you.

Lesson 5

Page 66, Exercise A

CD T-30

Dr. Hoffer: Nelson, I wonder if I could run a case past you?

Dr. Washington: Sure, Dave. Shoot.

Dr. Hoffer: OK, It's a 27-year-old woman who presented with otalgia and was referred to me for investigation of impacted eights. I noticed a small lesion, about 5mm in diameter, in the floor of the mouth and so when I was doing the 8s I did an excision biopsy of the lesion.

Dr. Washington: And it came back positive.

Dr. Hoffer: You got it! Moderately differentiated squamous cell carcinoma.

Dr. Washington: So, let me guess, the question is whether I think surgery is enough or if I would go for radiation or chemotherapy.

Dr. Hoffer: Right again.

Dr. Washington: OK. We're talking about a 5mm lesion with no cervical lymph nodes.

Dr. Hoffer: And with no invasion of the gingiva.

Dr. Washington: According to my experience, radiation or chemotherapy won't make any difference in the 5-year survival rate in a 5mm lesion and the side effects can severely affect the quality of life. If your excision biopsy had a good margin of healthy tissue, then I think your patient can be spared any more treatment.

Dr. Hoffer: That was exactly my plan. But it's always good to get a second opinion. Thanks, Nelson.